Soups & Appetizers

Practical
Step-by-Step
Collection

**FLAME TREE
PUBLISHING**

This is a Flame Tree book
First published in 2005
This edition 2011

11 13 15 14 12

1 3 5 7 9 10 8 6 4 2

Flame Tree Publishing is part of
The Foundry Creative Media Company Limited
Crabtree Hall, Crabtree Lane, Fulham, London, SW6 6TY

www.flametreepublishing.com

ISBN: 978-0-85775-148-5

The CIP record for this book is available from the British Library.

Printed in China

ACKNOWLEDGMENTS

Publisher and Creative Director: Nick Wells
Project Editor: Catherine Taylor
Original Editorial: Sarah Goulding
Design and Production: Chris Herbert, Mike Spender, Colin Rudderham, and Claire Walker

Authors: Catherine Atkinson, Juliet Barker, Gina Steer, Vicki Smallwood,
Carol Tennant, Mari Mererid Williams, Elizabeth Wolf-Cohen, and Simone Wright
Editorial: Gina Steer and Karen Fitzpatrick
Photography: Colin Bowling, Paul Forrester, and Stephen Brayne
Home Economists and Stylists: Jacqueline Bellefontaine,
Mandy Phipps, Vicki Smallwood, and Penny Stephens
Design Team: Helen Courtney, Jennifer Bishop, Lucy Bradbury, and Chris Herbert

All props supplied by Barbara Stewart at Surfaces

NOTE
Recipes using uncooked eggs should be avoided by infants,
the elderly, pregnant women, and anyone with a chronic illness.

Contents

Soups

Appetizers

Hygiene in the Kitchen

It is important to remember that many foods can carry some form of bacteria. In most cases, the worst it will lead to is a bout of food poisoning or gastroenteritis, but this can be serious for certain people. The risk can be reduced or eliminated, however, by good hygiene and proper cooking.

Do not buy food that is past its sell, or pull, date and do not consume food past its expiration date. When buying food, use your eyes and nose. If the food looks tired, limp, or a bad color or it has a rank, acrid, or bad smell, do not buy or eat it under any circumstances.

Be especially careful when preparing raw meat and fish. A separate cutting board should be used for each, and the knife, board, and your hands should be thoroughly washed before handling or preparing any other food.

Regularly clean, defrost, and clear out the refrigerator or freezer—it is worth checking the packaging to see exactly how long each product is safe to freeze. Avoid handling food if you have a stomach ache because bacteria can be passed on through food preparation.

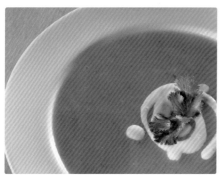

Dish towels must be washed and changed regularly. Ideally, use disposable cloths, which should be replaced on a daily basis. More durable cloths should be left to soak in bleach, then washed in the washing machine at a high temperature.

Keep your hands, cooking utensils, and food preparation surfaces clean and do not let pets climb onto any work counters.

Buying

Avoid bulk buying where possible, especially fresh produce, such as meat, poultry, fish, fruit, and vegetables. Fresh foods lose their nutritional value rapidly, so buying a little at a time minimizes loss of nutrients. It also means your refrigerator won't be so full, which reduces the effectiveness of the refrigeration process.

When buying prepared goods, such as cans or containers of cream and yogurts, check that the packaging is intact and not damaged or pierced. Cans should not be dented, pierced, or rusty. Check the expiration dates for cans and packages of dry ingredients, such as flour and rice. Store fresh foods in the refrigerator as soon as possible—not in the car or the office.

When buying frozen foods, make sure that they are not heavily iced on the outside and that the contents feel completely frozen. Make sure that the frozen foods have been stored in the cabinet at the correct storage level and the temperature is below -0.4°F. Pack in cooler bags to transport home and place in the freezer as soon as possible after purchase.

Preparation

Make sure that all work surfaces and utensils are clean and dry. Hygiene should be given priority at all times. Separate cutting boards should be used for raw and cooked meats, fish, and vegetables. Currently, a variety

of good-quality plastic boards come in various designs and colors. This makes differentiating easier and the plastic has the added hygienic advantage of being washable at high temperatures in the dishwasher. If using the board for fish, first wash in cold water, then in hot to prevent odor. Also remember that knives and utensils should always be thoroughly cleaned after use.

When cooking, be particularly careful to keep cooked and raw food separate to avoid any contamination. It is worth washing all fruits and vegetables regardless of whether they are going to be eaten raw or lightly cooked. This rule should apply even to packages of prewashed herbs and salads.

Do not reheat food more than once. If using a microwave, always check that the food is piping hot all the way through—in theory, the food should reach 158°F and needs to be cooked at that temperature for at least three minutes to make sure that all bacteria are killed.

All poultry must be thoroughly thawed before using, including chicken and poussin. Remove the food to be thawed from the freezer and place in a shallow dish to contain the juices. Leave the food in the refrigerator until it is completely thawed. A 3-pound whole chicken will take about 26–30 hours to thaw. To speed up the process, immerse the chicken in cold water, making sure that the water is changed regularly. When the pieces can move freely and no ice crystals remain in the cavity, the bird is completely thawed.

Once thawed, remove the packaging and pat the chicken dry. Place the chicken in a shallow dish, cover lightly, and store as close to the bottom of the refrigerator as possible. The chicken should be cooked as soon as possible.

Some foods can be cooked from frozen, including many prepared foods, such as soups, sauces, casseroles, and breads. Where applicable, follow the manufacturers' directions.

Vegetables and fruits can also be cooked from frozen, but meats and fish should be thawed first. The only time food can be refrozen is when the food has been thoroughly thawed, then cooked. Once the food has cooled, then it can be frozen again, but it should only be stored for one month.

All poultry and game (except for duck) must be cooked thoroughly. When cooked, the juices will run clear on the thickest part of the bird—the best area to try is usually the thigh. Other meats, such as ground meat and pork, should be cooked all the way through. Fish should turn opaque, be firm in texture, and break easily into large flakes.

When cooking leftovers, make sure they are reheated until piping hot and that any sauce or soup reaches boiling point first.

Storing, Refrigerating, and Freezing

Meat, poultry, fish, seafood, and dairy products should all be refrigerated. The temperature of the refrigerator should be between 34°F and 41°F, while the freezer temperature should not rise above -0.4°F.

To ensure the optimum refrigerator and freezer temperature, avoid leaving the door open for long periods of time. Try not to overstock the refrigerator because this reduces the airflow inside and, therefore, the effectiveness in cooling the food within.

When refrigerating cooked food, let it cool down quickly and completely before refrigerating. Hot food will raise the temperature of the refrigerator and possibly affect or spoil other food stored in it.

Food within the refrigerator and freezer should always be covered. Raw and cooked food should be stored in separate parts of the refrigerator. Cooked food should be kept on the top shelves of the refrigerator, while raw meat, poultry, and fish should be placed on bottom shelves to avoid drips and cross-contamination. It is

recommended that eggs should be refrigerated in order to maintain their freshness and shelf life.

Be careful that frozen foods are not kept stored in the freezer for too long. Blanched vegetables can be stored for one month; beef, lamb, poultry, and pork for six months; and unblanched vegetables and fruits in syrup for a year. Oily fish and sausages can be stored for three months. Dairy products can last four to six months, while cakes and pastries can be kept in the freezer for three to six months.

High-Risk Foods

Certain foods may carry risks to people who are considered vulnerable, such as the elderly, the ill, pregnant women, babies, young infants, and those people with a chronic illness.

It is advisable to avoid those foods listed below, which belong in a higher-risk category.

There is a slight chance that some eggs carry the bacteria salmonella. Cook the eggs until both the yolk and the white are firm to eliminate this risk. Pay particular attention to dishes and products incorporating lightly cooked or raw eggs, which should be eliminated from the diet. Hollandaise sauce, mayonnaise, mousses, soufflés, and meringues all use raw or lightly cooked eggs, as do custard-based dishes, ice creams, and sorbets. These are all considered high-risk foods to the vulnerable groups mentioned above.

Certain meats and poultry also carry the potential risk of salmonella and so should be cooked thoroughly until the juices run clear and there is no

pinkness left. Unpasteurized products, such as milk, cheese (especially soft cheese), pâté, and meat (both raw and cooked), all have the potential risk of listeria and should be avoided.

When buying seafood, buy from a reputable source that has a high turnover to ensure freshness. Fish should have bright clear eyes, shiny skin, and bright pink or red gills. The fish should feel stiff to the touch, with a slight smell of sea air and iodine. The flesh of fish steaks and fillets should be translucent with no signs of discoloration. Mollusks, such as scallops, clams, and mussels, are sold fresh and are still alive. Avoid any that are open or do not close when tapped lightly. In the same way, univalves, such as abalones or periwinkles, should withdraw back into their shells when lightly prodded. When choosing cephalopods, such as squid and octopus, they should have a firm flesh and pleasant sea smell.

As with all fish, whether it is shellfish or sea fish, care is required when freezing it. It is imperative to check whether the fish has been frozen before. If it has been frozen, then it should not be frozen again under any circumstances.

Nutrition The Role of Essential Nutrients

A healthy and well-balanced diet is the body's primary energy source. In children, it constitutes the building blocks for future health as well as providing a lot of energy. In adults, it encourages self-healing and regeneration within the body. A well-balanced diet will provide the body with all the essential nutrients it needs. This can be achieved by eating a variety of foods, demonstrated in the pyramid below.

FATS

PROTEINS

milk,   meat, fish,
yogurt,   poultry, eggs,
and cheese   nuts, and beans

FRUIT AND VEGETABLES

STARCHY CARBOHYDRATES

cereals, potatoes, bread, rice, and pasta

FATS

Fats fall into two categories: saturated and unsaturated. It is very important that a healthy balance is achieved within the diet. Fats are an essential part of the diet; they are a source of energy and provide essential fatty acids and fat soluble vitamins. The right balance of fats should boost the body's immunity to infection and keep muscles, nerves, and arteries in good condition. Saturated fats are of animal origin and are hard when stored at room temperature. They can be found in dairy produce, meat, eggs, margarines, and hard white cooking fat (lard) as well as in manufactured products, such as pies, cookies, and cakes. A high intake of saturated fat over many years has been proven to increase heart disease and high blood cholesterol levels and often leads to weight gain. The aim of a healthy diet is to keep the fat content low in the foods that we eat. Lowering the amount of saturated fat that we consume is very important, but this does not mean that it is good to consume a lot of other types of fat.

There are two kinds of unsaturated fats: polyunsaturated and monounsaturated. Polyunsaturated fats include safflower, soybean, corn, and sesame oils. Within the polyunsaturated group are Omega oils. The Omega-3 oils are of significant interest because they have been found to be particularly beneficial to coronary health and can encourage brain growth and development. Omega-3 oils are derived from oily fish, such as salmon, mackerel, herring, pilchards, and sardines. It is recommended that we should eat these types of fish at least once a week. However, for those who do not eat fish or who are vegetarians, liver oil supplements are available in most supermarkets and health food stores. It is suggested that these supplements should be taken on a daily basis. The most popular oils that are high in monounsaturates are olive oil, sunflower oil, and peanut oil. The Mediterranean diet, which is based on a diet high in monounsaturated fats, is recommended for heart health. Monounsaturated fats are also known to help reduce the levels of cholestrol.

PROTEINS

Composed of amino acids—proteins' building blocks—proteins perform a wide variety of essential functions for the body, including supplying energy and building and repairing tissues. Good sources of proteins are eggs, milk, yogurt, cheese, meat, fish, poultry, nuts, and beans. (See the second level of the pyramid.) Some of these foods, however, contain saturated fats. To strike a nutritional balance, eat generous amounts of vegetable protein foods, such as soybeans and other beans, lentils, peas, and nuts.

FRUIT AND VEGETABLES

Not only are fruit and vegetables the most visually appealing foods, but they are extremely good for us, providing essential vitamins and minerals essential for growth, repair, and protection in the human body. Fruit and vegetables are low in calories and are responsible for regulating the body's metabolic processes and controlling the composition of its fluids and cells.

MINERALS

CALCIUM Important for healthy bones and teeth, nerve transmission, muscle contraction, blood clotting, and hormone function. Calcium promotes a healthy heart, improves skin, relieves aching muscles and bones, maintains the correct acid-alkaline balance, and reduces menstrual cramps. Good sources are dairy products, small bones of small fish, nuts, beans, fortified white flours, breads, and green leafy vegetables.

CHROMIUM Part of the glucose tolerance factor, chromium balances blood sugar levels, helps to normalize hunger and reduce cravings, improves lifespan, helps protect DNA, and is essential for heart function. Good sources are brewer's yeast, whole-wheat bread, rye bread, oysters, potatoes, green bell peppers, butter, and parsnips.

IODINE Important for the manufacture of thyroid hormones and for normal development. Good sources of iodine are seafood, seaweed, milk, and dairy products.

IRON As a component of hemoglobin, iron carries oxygen around the body. It is vital for normal growth and development. Good sources are liver, corned beef, red meat, fortified breakfast cereals, beans, green leafy vegetables, egg yolk, and cocoa and cocoa products.

MAGNESIUM Important for efficient functioning of metabolic enzymes and development of the skeleton. Magnesium promotes healthy muscles by helping them to relax and is, therefore, good for premenstrual syndrome (PMS). It is also important for heart muscles and the nervous system. Good sources are nuts, green vegetables, meat, cereals, milk, and yogurt.

PHOSPHORUS Forms and maintains bones and teeth, builds muscle tissue, helps maintain pH of the body, and aids metabolism and energy production. Phosphorus is present in almost all foods.

POTASSIUM Enables nutrients to move into cells while waste products move out; promotes healthy nerves and muscles; maintains fluid balance in the body; helps secretion of insulin for blood sugar control to produce constant energy; relaxes muscles; maintains heart functioning; and stimulates digestive movement to encourage elimination. Good sources are fruit, vegetables, milk, and bread.

SELENIUM Antioxidant properties help to protect against free radicals and carcinogens. Selenium reduces inflammation, stimulates the immune system to fight infections, promotes a healthy heart, and helps vitamin E's action. It is also required for the male reproductive system and is needed for metabolism. Good sources are tuna, liver, kidney, meat, eggs, cereals, nuts, and dairy products.

SODIUM Important in helping to control body fluid and balance, preventing dehydration. Sodium is involved in muscle and nerve function and helps move nutrients into cells. All foods are good sources. Processed, pickled, and salted foods are richest in sodium but should be eaten in moderation.

ZINC Important for metabolism and the healing of wounds. It also aids ability to cope with stress, promotes a healthy nervous system and brain, especially in the growing fetus, aids bone and teeth formation, and is essential for constant energy. Good sources are liver, meat, beans, whole-grain cereals, nuts, and oysters.

VITAMINS

VITAMIN A Important for cell growth and development and for the formation of visual pigments in the eye. Vitamin A comes in two forms: retinol and beta-carotenes. Retinol is found in liver, meat and meat products, and whole milk and its products. Beta-carotene is a powerful antioxidant and is found in red and yellow fruits and vegetables, such as carrots, mangoes, and apricots.

VITAMIN B1 Important in releasing energy from carbohydrate-containing foods. Good sources are yeast and yeast products, bread, fortified breakfast cereals, and potatoes.

VITAMIN B2 Important for metabolism of proteins, fats, and carbohydrates to produce energy. Good sources are meat, yeast extracts, fortified breakfast cereals, and milk and its products.

VITAMIN B3 Required for the metabolism of food into energy production. Good sources are milk and milk products, fortified breakfast cereals, beans, meat, poultry, and eggs.

VITAMIN B5 Important for the metabolism of food and energy production. All foods are good sources but especially fortified breakfast cereals, whole-grain bread, and dairy products.

VITAMIN B6 Important for metabolism of protein and fat. Vitamin B6 may also be involved in the regulation of sex hormones. Good sources are liver, fish, pork, soybeans, and peanuts.

VITAMIN B12 Important for the production of red blood cells and DNA. It is vital for growth and the nervous system. Good sources are meat, fish, eggs, poultry, and milk.

BIOTIN Important for metabolism of fatty acids. Good sources of biotin are liver, kidney, eggs, and nuts. Microorganisms also manufacture this vitamin in the digestive system.

VITAMIN C Important for healing wounds and the formation of collagen, which keeps skin and bones strong. It is an important antioxidant. Good sources are fruits, especially berries, and vegetables.

VITAMIN D Important for absorption and handling of calcium to help build bone strength. Good sources are oily fish, eggs, whole milk and milk products, margarine, and, of course, sufficient exposure to sunlight, because vitamin D is made in the skin.

VITAMIN E Important as an antioxidant vitamin helping to protect cell membranes from damage. Good sources are vegetable oils, margarines, seeds, nuts, and green vegetables.

FOLIC ACID Critical during pregnancy for the development of the brain and nerves. It is always essential for brain and nerve function and is needed for utilizing protein and red blood cell formation. Good sources are whole-grain cereals, fortified breakfast cereals, green leafy vegetables, oranges, and liver.

VITAMIN K Important for controlling blood clotting. Good sources are cauliflower, Brussels sprouts, lettuce, cabbage, beans, broccoli, peas, asparagus, potatoes, corn oil, tomatoes, and milk.

CARBOHYDRATES

Carbohydrates are an energy source and come in two forms: starch and sugar. Starch carbohydrates are also known as complex carbohydrates and they include all cereals, potatoes, breads, rice, and pasta. (See the fourth level of the pyramid). Eating whole-grain varieties of these foods also provides fiber. Diets high in fiber are believed to be beneficial in helping to prevent bowel cancer and can also keep cholesterol down. High-fiber diets are also good for those concerned about weight gain. Fiber is bulky and fills the stomach, therefore, reducing hunger pangs. Sugar carbohydrates, which are also known as fast-release carbohydrates because of the quick fix of energy they give to the body, include sugar and sugar-sweetened products, such as jellies and syrups. Milk provides lactose, which is a milk sugar, and fruits provide fructose, which is a fruit sugar.

Guidelines for Different Age Groups

Good food plays such an important role in everyone's life. From infancy through to adulthood, a healthy diet provides the body's foundation and building blocks and teaches children healthy eating habits. Studies have shown that these eating habits stay with us into later life helping us to maintain a healthier lifestyle as adults. This reduces the risk of illness, disease, and certain medical problems.

Striking a healthy balance is important and, at certain stages in life, this balance may need to be adjusted to help our bodies cope. As

babies and children, during pregnancy, and in later life, our diet assists us in achieving optimal health. So, how do we go about achieving this?

We know that a food such as oily fish, for example, is advantageous to all, because it is rich in Omega-3 fatty acids that have been linked with more efficient brain functioning and better memory. They can also help lower the risk of cancer and heart disease. However, are there any other steps we can take to maximize health benefits through our diet?

Babies and Young children

Babies should not be given solids until they are at least six months old, then new tastes and textures can be introduced to their diets. Probably the easiest and cheapest way is to adapt the food that the rest of the family eat. Babies under the age of one should be given breast milk or formula milk. From the age of one to two, whole milk should be given, and from two to five low-fat milk can be given. From then on, skim milk can be introduced, if desired.

The first foods for babies under six months should be of a pureelike consistency, which is smooth and fairly liquid, therefore, making it easy to swallow. This can be done using an electric blender or immersion blender or just by pushing foods through a strainer to remove any lumps. Remember that babies still need high levels of milk.

Babies over six months old should still be having pureed food, but the consistency of their diet can be made progressively lumpier. Around the 10-month mark, most babies can manage food cut up into small pieces.

So, what food groups do babies and small children need? Like adults, a high proportion of their diet should contain grains, such as cereal, pasta, bread, and rice. Be careful, however, because babies and small children cannot

cope with too much high-fiber foods in their diet.

Fresh fruit and vegetables should be introduced, as well as a balance of dairy and meat proteins and only a small proportion of fats and candy. Research points out that delaying the introduction of foods that could cause allergies during the first year (such as cow's milk, wheat, eggs, cheese, yogurt, and nuts) can significantly reduce the risk of certain food allergies later on in life. (NB: Peanuts should never be given to children under five years old.)

Seek a pediatrician's or nurse's advice regarding babies and toddlers. Limit sugar in young children's diets because it provides only empty calories. Use less processed sugars or incorporate less refined alternatives, such as dried fruits, dates, rice syrup, or honey. (NB: Honey should not be given to infants under one year of age.)

As in a low-fat diet, it is best to eliminate fried foods and avoid adding salt—especially for under one year olds and young infants. Instead, introduce herbs and gentle spices to make food appetizing. The more varied the tastes that children experience in their formative years, the wider the range of foods they will accept later in life.

Pregnancy

During pregnancy, women are advised to take extra vitamin and mineral supplements. Pregnant women benefit from a healthy balanced diet, rich in fresh fruit and vegetables and full of essential vitamins and minerals. Oily fish, such as salmon, not only give the body essential fats but also provide high levels of bio-available calcium.

Certain food groups, however, hold risks during pregnancy. This section gives advice on everyday foods and those that should be avoided.

Cheese

Pregnant women should avoid all soft mold-ripened cheese, such as Brie. Also, if pregnant, do not eat cheese, including Stilton and Danish Blue, because they carry the risk of potential listeria. It is fine for pregnant women to carry on eating hard cheese, such as American or cheddar cheese, as well as cottage cheese.

Eggs

There is a slight chance that some eggs will carry salmonella. Cooking the eggs until both the yolk and white are firm will eliminate this risk. However, particular attention should be paid to dishes and products that incorporate lightly cooked or raw eggs, homemade mayonnaise or similar sauces, mousses, soufflés, meringues, ice cream, and sorbets. Commercially produced products, such as mayonnaise, which are made with pasteurized eggs may be eaten safely. If in doubt, play safe and avoid it.

Prepared meals and ingredients

Previously cooked, then chilled meals are now available, but those from the refrigerated section of the grocery store can contain bacteria. Avoid prepared salads in dressings and other foods that are sold loose in the refrigerated sections. Do not eat raw or partially cooked meats, pâté, unpasteurized milk, and soil-dirty fruit and vegetables because they can cause toxoplasmosis.

Meat and fish

Certain meats and poultry carry the potential risk of salmonella and should be cooked thoroughly until the juices run clear and there is no pinkness left.

Pay particular attention when buying and cooking fish (especially shellfish). Buy only the freshest fish, which should smell salty but not strong or fishy.

Look for bright eyes and reject any with sunken eyes. The bodies should look fresh, plump, and shiny. Avoid any fish with dry, shriveled, or damp bodies.

It is also best to avoid any shellfish while pregnant unless it is definitely fresh and thoroughly cooked. Shellfish also contains harmful bacteria and viruses.

Later life

So what about later on in life? As the body gets older, we can help stave off infection and illness through our diet. There is evidence to show that the immune system becomes weaker as we get older, which can increase the risk of developing cancer and other illnesses. Maintaining a diet rich in antioxidants, fresh fruit and vegetables, plant oils, and oily fish is especially beneficial in order to either prevent these illnesses or minimize their effects. As with all age groups, the body benefits from the five-a-day eating plan—try to eat five portions of fruit or vegetables each day. Leafy green vegetables, in particular, are rich in antioxidants. Cabbage, broccoli, Brussels sprouts, cauliflower, and kale contain particularly high levels of antioxidants, which lower the risk of cancer.

Foods that are green in color tend to provide nutrients essential for healthy nerves, muscles, and hormones, while foods red in color protect against cardiovascular disease. Other foods that can also assist in preventing cardiovascular disease and ensuring a healthy heart include vitamins E and C, oily fish, and essential fats (such as extra-virgin olive oil and garlic). They help lower blood cholesterol levels and clear arteries. A diet high in fresh fruit and vegetables and low in salt and saturated fats can considerably reduce heart disease.

Other foods have recognized properties. Certain types of mushrooms are known to boost the immune system, while garlic not only boosts the immune system but also protects the body against cancer. Live yogurt, too, has healthy properties because it contains friendly bacteria that help digestion.

Some foods can help to balance the body's hormone levels during the menopause. For example, soy products regulate hormone levels. Studies have shown that a regular intake of soy products can help to protect the body against breast and prostate cancer.

A balanced, healthy diet, rich in fresh fruit and vegetables, carbohydrates, proteins, and essential fats and low in saturates, can help the body protect itself throughout its life. It really is worth spending a little extra time and effort when shopping or even just thinking about what to cook.

Pantry Essentials
Ingredients for a Healthy Lifestyle

With the increasing emphasis on the importance of cooking healthy meals for your family, modern lifestyles are naturally shifting toward lower-fat and cholesterol diets. Low-fat cooking has often been associated with the idea that reducing fat reduces flavor, but this simply is not the case, which is great news for those trying to eat healthily. Thanks to the increasing number of lower-fat ingredients now available in grocery stores, there is no need to compromise on the choice of foods we eat.

The pantry is a good place to start when cooking healthy meals. Most of us have fairly limited cooking and preparation time available during the week, and so choose to experiment during weekends. When time is of the essence, or friends arrive unannounced, it is a good idea to have some well thought-out basics in the pantry, namely foods that are high on flavor while still being healthy.

Because pantry ingredients keep reasonably well, it is worth making a trip to a good specialty grocery store. Our society's growing interest in recent years with travel and food from around the world has led us to seek out alternative ingredients with which to experiment and incorporate into our cooking. Consequently, supermarket chains have had to broaden their product range and often have a specialty range of imported ingredients from around the world.

If the local grocers or supermarket only carries a limited choice of products, do not worry. The internet now offers freedom to food lovers. There are some fantastic food sites (both local and international), where food can be purchased

and delivery arranged online.

When thinking about essentials, think of flavor, something that is going to add to a dish without increasing its fat content. It is worth spending a little bit more money on these products to make flavorsome dishes that will help stop the urge to snack on fatty foods.

Pantry Hints

There are many different types of pantry ingredients readily available—including myriad varieties of rice and pasta—which can provide much of the carbohydrate required in our daily diets. Store the ingredients in a cool, dark place and remember to rotate them. The ingredients will be safe to use for six months.

Bulgur wheat A cracked wheat that is often used in tabbouleh. Bulgur wheat is a good source of complex carbohydrate.

Couscous Now available in instant form, couscous just needs to be covered with boiling water, then forked. Couscous is a precooked wheat semolina. Traditional couscous needs to be steamed and is available from health food stores. This type of couscous contains more nutrients than the instant variety.

Dried fruit The ready-to-eat variety are particularly good because they are plump, juicy, and do not need to be soaked. They are fantastic when pureed into a compote, added to water and heated to make a pie filling, and when added to stuffing mixtures. They are also good cooked with meats, rice, or couscous.

Flours A useful addition (particularly cornstarch) that can be used to thicken

sauces. It is worth mentioning that whole-grain flour should not be stored for too long at room temperature because the fats may turn rancid. While not a flour, cornmeal is a versatile low-fat ingredient that can be used when making dumplings and gnocchi.

Noodles Also useful and can accompany any Far Eastern dish. They are low in fat and also available in the whole-wheat variety. Rice noodles are available for those who have gluten-free diets and, like pasta noodles, provide slow-release energy to the body.

Pasta It is good to have a mixture of whole-wheat and plain pasta, as well as a wide variety of flavored pastas. Whether fresh (it can also be frozen) or dried, pasta is a versatile ingredient with which to provide the body with slow-release energy. It comes in many different sizes and shapes, from the tiny tubettini (which can be added to soups to create a more substantial dish), to penne, fusilli, rigatoni, and conchiglie, up to the larger cannelloni and lasagne noodles.

Hulled and pearl barley Hulled barley has only the husk removed, whereas pearl barley has also been steamed and polished; hulled barley is the most nutritious form. A high cereal diet can help prevent bowel diseases.

Beans A vital ingredient for the pantry, beans are easy to store, have a very high nutritional value, and are great when added to soups, casseroles, curries, and stews. Beans also act as a thickener, whether flavored or on their own. They come in two forms: either dried (in which case they generally need to be soaked overnight and then cooked before use—it is important to follow the directions on the back of the package), or canned, which is a convenient timesaver because the preparation of dried beans can take a while. If buying canned beans, try to buy those in water with no added salt or sugar. These simply need to be drained and rinsed before being added to a dish.

Kidney, borlotti, cannellini, lima, and flageolet beans, chickpeas, split peas, and lentils all make tasty additions to any dish. Baked beans are a favorite with everyone and many stores now stock the organic type, which have no added salt or sugar but are sweetened with fruit juice instead.

When boiling previously dried beans, remember that salt should not be added because this will make the skins tough and inedible. French green lentils (sometimes called Puy lentils) are a smaller type. They often have mottled skins and are good for cooking in slow dishes because they hold their shape and firm texture particularly well.

Rice Basmati and jasmine rices are well suited to Thai and Indian curries, because the fine grains absorb the sauce and their delicate creaminess balances the pungency of the spices.

Arborio is only one type of risotto rice; in Italy, many are available, depending on whether the risotto is meant to accompany meat, fish, or vegetable dishes. When cooked, rice swells to create a substantial low-fat dish. Regular white or brown rice is great for casseroles and for stuffing meat, fish, and vegetables, because it holds its shape and firmness. Short-grain rice can be used in a variety of ways to create an irresistible dessert.

Stock Good-quality stock is a must in cooking because it provides an excellent flavor base for many dishes. Many supermarkets now carry a variety of fresh and organic stocks, and although they need refrigeration, they are one of the most time- and effort-saving ingredients available. There is also a large range of dried stock, perhaps the best being bouillon, a high-quality form of stock (available in powder or liquid form), which can be added to any dish whether it be a sauce, casserole, pie, or soup.

Many people favor meals that can be prepared and cooked in as little as 30–45 minutes, so helpful ingredients that jump-start a sauce are great. A good-quality tomato puree or canned crushed tomatoes can act as the foundation for any sauce, as can a good-quality green or red pesto. Other handy pantry additions include tapenade, mustard, and anchovies. These ingredients have very distinctive tastes and are particularly flavorsome. Roasted red bell pepper sauce and sundried tomato paste, which tends to be sweeter and more intensely flavored than regular tomato paste, are also very useful.

Vinegar is another worthwhile pantry essential and, with so many uses, it is worth splashing out on really good quality balsamic and wine vinegars. Herbs and spices are also a must. Using herbs when cooking at home should reduce the temptation to buy prepared sauces. Often these types of sauces contain large amounts of sugar and additives.

Yeast extract is also a good pantry ingredient, because it can pep up sauces, soups, and casseroles and adds a little substance, particularly to vegetarian dishes.

Eastern flavors can offer a lot of scope where low-fat cooking is concerned. Flavorings such as Thai fish sauce, soy sauce, red and green curry pastes, and Chinese rice wine all offer mouthwatering, low-fat flavors to that can be easily adapted to other cuisines.

For those who are incredibly short on time, or who rarely shop, it is now possible to purchase a selection of already-prepared, freshly minced garlic, ginger, and chile. These are available in jars that can be kept in the refrigerator.

As well as these pantry additions, many grocery stores and especially supermarkets provide a wide choice of foods. Where possible, invest in the leanest cut of meat and substitute saturated fats, such as cream, butter, and cheese, with low-fat or reduced-fat alternatives.

Herbs and Spices

Herbs are easy to grow, and a garden is not needed because they can easily thrive on a small patio, in a window box, or even on a windowsill. It is worth the effort to plant a few herbs because they do not require much attention or nurturing. The reward will be a range of fresh herbs available whenever needed, and fresh flavors that cannot be beaten to add to any dish that is being prepared.

While fresh herbs should be picked or bought as close as possible to the time of use, freeze-dried and dried herbs and spices will usually keep for around six months.

The best idea is to buy little and often, and to store the herbs in airtight jars in a cool, dark cupboard. Fresh herbs tend to have a milder flavor than dried and equate to around one level tablespoon of fresh to one level teaspoon of dried. As a result, quantities used in cooking should be altered accordingly. A variety of herbs and spices and their uses are listed below.

ALLSPICE
The dark allspice berries come whole or ground and have a flavor similar to that of cinnamon, cloves, and nutmeg. Although not the same as apple pie or pumpkin spices, allspice can be used with pickles, relishes, cakes, and milk puddings or whole in meat and fish dishes.

ANISE SEED
Anise seed comes in whole seeds or ground. It has a strong aroma and flavor and should be used sparingly in baking and salad dressings.

BASIL

Best fresh but also available in dried form, basil can be used raw or cooked. It works well in many dishes but is particularly well suited to tomato-base dishes and sauces, salads, and Mediterranean recipes.

BAY LEAVES
Bay leaves are available in fresh or dried form as well as ground. They make up part of a bouquet garni and are particularly delicious when added to meat and poultry dishes, soups, stews, vegetable dishes, and stuffing. They also impart a spicy flavor to milk puddings and egg custards.

BOUQUET GARNI
Bouquet garni is a bouquet of fresh herbs tied with a piece of string or in a small piece of cheesecloth. It is used to flavor casseroles, stews, stocks, and sauces. The herbs that are normally used are parsley, thyme, and bay leaves.

CARAWAY SEEDS
Caraway seeds have a warm sweet taste and are often used in breads and cakes, but they are delicious with cabbage dishes and pickles as well.

CAYENNE
Cayenne is the powdered form of a red chile pepper said to be native to Cayenne. It is similar in appearance to paprika and can be used sparingly to add a fiery kick to many dishes.

CARDAMOM
Cardamom has a distinctive sweet, rich taste and can be bought whole in the pod, in seed form, or ground. This sweet aromatic spice is delicious in curries, rice, cakes, and cookies and is great served with rice pudding and fruit.

CHERVIL
Reminiscent of parsley and available either in fresh or dried form, chervil has a faintly sweet, spicy flavor and is particularly good in soups, cheese dishes, stews, and with eggs.

CHILE
Available whole, fresh, dried, and in powdered form, red chiles tend to be sweeter in taste than their green counterparts. They are particularly associated with Spanish and Mexican-style cooking and curries, but are also delicious with pickles, dips, sauces, and in pizza toppings.

CHIVES
Best used when fresh but also available in dried form, this member of the onion family is ideal for use when a delicate onion flavor is required. Chives are good with eggs, cheese, fish, and vegetable dishes. They also work well as a garnish for soups, meat, and vegetable dishes.

CINNAMON
Cinnamon comes in the form of reddish brown sticks of bark from an evergreen tree and has a sweet, pungent aroma. Either whole or ground, cinnamon is delicious in cakes and milk puddings, particularly with apple, and is used in mulled wine and for preserving.

CLOVES
Mainly used whole although also available ground, cloves have a very warm, sweet pungent aroma and can be used to stud roasted ham and pork, in mulled wine and punch, and when pickling fruit. When ground, they can be used in making mincemeat pie and in Christmas puddings and cookies.

CORIANDER/CILANTRO
Coriander seeds have an orangey flavor and are available whole or ground. Coriander is particularly delicious (whether whole or roughly ground) in casseroles, curries, and as a pickling spice. The leaves are known as cilantro and are used to flavor spicy aromatic dishes as well as a garnish.

CUMIN
Also available ground or as whole seeds, cumin has a strong, slightly bitter flavor. It is one of the main ingredients in curry powder and compliments many fish, meat, and rice dishes.

DILL
Dill weed—the dill leaves—are available fresh or dried and have a mild flavor, while the seeds are slightly bitter. Dill is particularly good with salmon, new potatoes, and in sauces. The seeds are good in pickles and vegetable dishes.

FENNEL
Whole seeds or ground, fennel has a fragrant, sweet anise-seed flavor and is sometimes known as the fish herb because it compliments fish dishes so well.

GINGER
Ginger comes in many forms but primarily as a fresh root and in dried ground form, which can be used in baking, curries, pickles, sauces, and Chinese cooking.

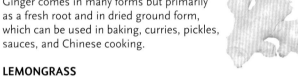

LEMONGRASS
Available fresh and dried, with a subtle, aromatic, lemony flavor, lemongrass is essential to Thai cooking. It is also delicious when added to soups, poultry, and fish dishes.

MACE
The outer husk of nutmeg has a milder nutmeg flavor and can be used in pickles, cheese dishes, stewed fruits, sauces, and hot punch.

MARJORAM
Often dried, marjoram has a sweet slightly spicy flavor, which tastes fantastic when added to stuffing, meat, or tomato-base dishes.

MINT
Available fresh or dried, mint has a strong, sweet aroma that is delicious in a sauce or jelly to serve with lamb. It is also great with fresh peas and new potatoes and is often added as a flavoring to beverages.

MUSTARD SEED
These yellow and brown seeds are available whole or ground and are often found in pickles, relishes, cheese dishes, dressings, curries, and as an accompaniment to meat.

NUTMEG
The large whole seeds have a warm, sweet taste and compliment custards, milk puddings, cheese dishes, parsnips, and creamy soups.

OREGANO
The strongly flavored dried leaves of oregano are similar to marjoram and are used extensively in Italian and Greek cooking.

PAPRIKA
Paprika often comes in two varieties. One is sweet and mild and the other has a slight bite to it. Paprika is made from the fruit of the sweet pepper and is good in meat and poultry dishes as well as a garnish. The rule of buying herbs and spices little and often applies particularly to paprika because, unfortunately, it does not keep particularly well.

PARSLEY
The stems as well as the leaves of parsley can be used to compliment most savory dishes because they contain the most flavor. They can also be used as a garnish.

PEPPER
This comes in white and black peppercorns and is best freshly ground. Both add flavor to most dishes, sauces, and gravies. Black pepper has a more robust flavor, while white pepper is much more delicate.

POPPY SEEDS
These little, gray-black seeds impart a sweet, nutty flavor when added to cookies, bagels, vegetable dishes, dressings, and cheese dishes.

ROSEMARY
Delicious fresh or dried, these small, needlelike leaves have a sweet aroma that is particularly good with lamb, stuffing, and vegetables dishes. Also delicious when added to charcoal on the barbecue to add a piquant flavor to meat and corn on the cob.

SAFFRON
Deep orange in color, saffron is traditionally used in paella and other rice dishes and cakes but is also delicious with poultry. Saffron is the most expensive of all spices.

SAGE
Fresh or dried sage leaves have a pungent, slightly bitter taste that is delicious with pork and poultry, sausages, stuffing, and with stuffed pasta when tossed in a little butter and fresh sage.

SAVORY
This herb resembles thyme, but has a softer flavor that particularly compliments all types of fish and beans.

SESAME
Sesame seeds have a nutty taste, especially when toasted, and are delicious in baking, on salads, or with Asian cooking.

TARRAGON
The fresh or dried leaves of tarragon have a sweet aromatic taste that is particularly good with poultry, seafood, fish, creamy sauces, and stuffing.

THYME
Available fresh or dried, thyme has a pungent flavor and is included in bouquet garni. It compliments many meat and poultry dishes and stuffing.

TURMERIC
The bright yellow root of a lily from southeast Asia is ground up to make turmeric. It has a bitter, peppery flavor and is often combined for use in curry powder and mustard. Turmeric also makes a delicious addition to pickles, relishes, and dressings.

Soups

The wide range of soups provided in this section can serve as appetizers or full meals. Choose from clear or creamy recipes, sweet or spicy flavors, meat or vegetarian options. Whatever soup fits your needs, our comprehensive, straightforward recipes are sure to aid you in creating a delectable dish.

Mushroom & Sherry Soup

INGREDIENTS

Serves 4

4 slices day-old white bread

1 tsp. lemon zest

1 tbsp. lemon juice

salt and freshly ground black pepper

1¾ cups lightly rinsed assorted
  wild mushrooms

1¾ cups wiped baby mushrooms

2 tsp. olive oil

1 garlic clove, peeled and crushed

6 scallions, trimmed
  and diagonally sliced

2½ cups chicken stock

4 tbsp. dry sherry

1 tbsp. freshly cut chives, to garnish

HELPFUL HINT

To achieve very fine shreds, use a zester, available from all kitchen stores. Or, thinly peel the fruit with a vegetable peeler, then shred with a small, sharp knife. When grating fruit, use a clean, dry pastry brush to remove the rind from the grater.

1 Preheat the oven to 350°F. Remove the crusts from the bread and cut the bread into small cubes.

2 In a large bowl, toss the cubes of bread with the lemon zest and juice, 2 tablespoons water, and plenty of freshly ground black pepper.

3 Spread the bread cubes onto a lightly greased baking sheet and cook in the preheated oven for 20 minutes until golden and crisp.

4 If the wild mushrooms are small, leave some whole. Otherwise, thinly slice all the mushrooms and set aside.

5 Heat the olive oil in a saucepan. Add the garlic and scallions, and cook for 1–2 minutes.

6 Add the mushrooms and cook for 3–4 minutes until they start to soften. Add the chicken stock and stir to mix.

7 Bring to a boil, then reduce the heat to a gentle simmer. Cover the pan with a lid and cook for 10 minutes.

8 Stir in the sherry, and season to taste with a little salt and pepper. Pour into warmed bowls, sprinkle the chives on top, and serve the soup immediately with the lemon croutons.

2

4

6

Carrot & Ginger Soup

INGREDIENTS

Serves 4

4 slices bread, crusts removed
1 tsp. yeast extract
2 tsp. olive oil
1 onion, peeled and chopped
1 garlic clove, peeled and crushed
$\frac{1}{2}$ tsp. ground ginger
$2\frac{1}{2}$ cups peeled and chopped carrots
4 cups vegetable stock
1-in. piece fresh ginger, peeled and
  finely grated
salt and freshly ground black pepper
1 tbsp. lemon juice

To garnish:
chives
lemon zest

1 Preheat the oven to 350°F. Coarsely chop the bread. Dissolve the yeast extract in 2 tablespoons of warm water, and mix with the bread.

2 Spread the bread cubes over a lightly greased baking sheet and cook for 20 minutes, turning halfway through. Remove from the oven and set aside.

3 Heat the olive oil in a large saucepan. Gently cook the onion and garlic for 3–4 minutes.

4 Stir in the ground ginger and cook for 1 minute to release the flavor.

5 Add the chopped carrots, then stir in the stock and the fresh ginger. Simmer gently for 15 minutes.

6 Remove from the heat and let cool slightly. Blend until smooth, then season to taste with salt and pepper. Stir in the lemon juice. Garnish with the chives and lemon zest, and serve immediately.

TASTY TIP

For special occasions, serve with a spoonful of lightly whipped cream or créme fraîche.

2

4

6

Italian Bean Soup

INGREDIENTS

Serves 4

2 tsp. olive oil

1 leek, washed and chopped

1 garlic clove, peeled and crushed

2 tsp. dried oregano

³/₄ cup trimmed, bite-sized pieces
   green beans

14 oz. canned lima beans, drained
   and rinsed

³/₄ cup small pasta shapes

4 cups vegetable stock

8 cherry tomatoes

salt and freshly ground black pepper

3 tbsp. freshly torn basil

1 Heat the olive oil in a large saucepan. Add the leek, garlic, and oregano, and cook for 5 minutes, stirring occasionally.

2 Stir in the green beans and the lima beans. Sprinkle in the pasta and pour in the stock.

3 Bring the stock mixture to a boil, then reduce the heat to a simmer.

4 Cook for 12–15 minutes, or until the vegetables are tender and the pasta is cooked to al dente. Stir occasionally.

5 In a heavy skillet, fry the tomatoes over high heat until they soften and the skins begin to blacken.

6 Gently crush the tomatoes in the skillet with the back of a spoon, and add to the soup.

7 Season to taste with salt and pepper. Stir in the torn basil and serve immediately.

TASTY TIP

This soup will taste even better the day after it has been made. Make the soup the day before you intend to serve it, and add a little extra stock when reheating.

2

5

6

Tomato & Basil Soup

INGREDIENTS

Serves 4

7 medium, ripe tomatoes, cut in half
2 garlic cloves
1 tsp. olive oil
1 tbsp. balsamic vinegar
1 tbsp. dark brown sugar
1 tbsp. tomato paste
1¼ cups vegetable stock
6 tbsp. low-fat plain yogurt
2 tbsp. freshly chopped basil
salt and freshly ground black pepper
small fresh basil leaves, to garnish

TASTY TIP

Use the sweetest type of tomatoes available, as it makes a big difference to the flavor of the soup. Many supermarkets now stock special tomatoes, grown slowly and matured for longer on the vine to give them an intense flavor. If these are unavailable, add a little extra sugar to bring out the flavor.

1 Preheat the oven to 400°F. Evenly spread the tomato halves and unpeeled garlic in a single layer in a large roasting pan.

2 Mix the olive oil and vinegar together. Drizzle over the tomatoes and sprinkle with the dark brown sugar.

3 Roast the tomatoes in the preheated oven for 20 minutes until tender and lightly charred in places.

4 Remove from the oven and let cool slightly. When cool enough to handle, squeeze the softened flesh of the garlic from the papery skin. Place with the charred tomatoes in a strainer over a saucepan.

5 Press the garlic and tomato through the strainer with the back of a wooden spoon.

6 When all the flesh has been strained, add the tomato paste and the vegetable stock to the pan. Heat gently, stirring occasionally.

7 In a small bowl, beat the yogurt and basil together, and season to taste with salt and pepper. Stir the basil yogurt into the soup. Garnish with basil leaves and serve immediately.

2

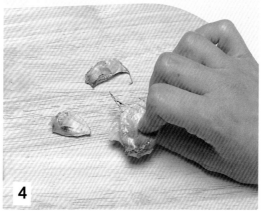
4

7

Curried Parsnip Soup

INGREDIENTS

Serves 4

1 tsp. cumin seeds
2 tsp. coriander seeds
1 tsp. oil
1 onion, peeled and chopped
1 garlic clove, peeled and crushed
$1/2$ tsp. turmeric
$1/4$ tsp. chili powder
1 cinnamon stick
2 cups peeled and chopped parsnips
4 cups vegetable stock
salt and freshly ground black pepper
fresh cilantro leaves, to garnish
2–3 tbsp. low-fat plain yogurt,
  to serve

1 In a small skillet, fry the cumin and coriander seeds over moderately high heat for 1–2 minutes. Shake the skillet during cooking until the seeds are lightly toasted.

2 Set aside until cooled. Grind toasted seeds with a mortar and pestle.

3 Heat the oil in a saucepan. Cook the onion until softened and starting to turn golden.

4 Add the garlic, turmeric, chili powder, and cinnamon stick to the pan. Continue to cook for an additional minute.

5 Add the parsnips and stir well. Pour in the stock and bring to a boil. Cover and simmer for 15 minutes, or until the parsnips are cooked.

6 Let the soup cool. Once cooled, remove the cinnamon stick and discard.

7 Blend the soup in a food processor until very smooth.

8 Transfer to a saucepan and reheat gently. Season to taste with salt and pepper. Garnish with fresh cilantro leaves and serve immediately with yogurt.

FOOD FACT

Parsnips vary in color from pale yellow to a creamy white. They are at their best when they are the size of a large carrot. If larger, remove central core, which can be woody.

Roasted Red Pepper, Tomato & Red Onion Soup

INGREDIENTS

Serves 4

fine spray of oil

2 large red bell peppers,
  seeded and coarsely chopped

1 red onion, peeled and
  coarsely chopped

2 medium tomatoes, halved

1 small, crusty French loaf

1 garlic clove, peeled

2½ cups vegetable stock

salt and freshly ground black pepper

1 tsp. Worcestershire sauce

4 tbsp. low-fat sour cream

HELPFUL HINT

A quick way to remove the skin from bell peppers once they have been roasted or broiled is to place them in a plastic bag. Leave for 10 minutes, or until cool enough to handle, then peel the skin away from the flesh.

1 Preheat the oven to 375°F. Spray a large roasting pan with the oil, and place the bell peppers and the onion in the base. Cook in the preheated oven for 10 minutes. Add the tomatoes and cook for an additional 20 minutes, or until the bell peppers are soft.

2 Cut the bread into slices ½ inch thick. Cut the garlic clove in half and rub the cut edge of the garlic over the bread.

3 Place all the bread slices on a large cookie sheet and cook in the oven for 10 minutes, turning halfway through, until golden and crisp.

4 Remove the vegetables from the oven and let it cool slightly, then blend in a food processor until smooth. Strain the vegetable mixture through a large strainer into a saucepan to remove the seeds and skin. Add the stock, season to taste with salt and pepper, and stir to mix. Heat the soup gently until piping hot.

5 In a small bowl, beat together the Worcestershire sauce with the sour cream.

6 Pour the soup into warmed bowls and swirl a spoonful of the sour cream mixture into each bowl. Serve immediately with the garlic toast.

1

4

5

Rutabaga, Turnip, Parsnip & Potato Soup

INGREDIENTS

Serves 4

2 large onions, peeled

2 tbsp. butter

2 medium carrots, peeled and
coarsely chopped

1 cup peeled and coarsely
chopped rutabaga

³/₄ cup peeled and coarsely
chopped turnip

³/₄ cup peeled and coarsely
chopped parsnips

1 cup peeled and coarsely
chopped potatoes

4¹/₄ cups vegetable stock

¹/₂ tsp. freshly grated nutmeg

salt and freshly ground black pepper

4 tbsp. vegetable oil, for frying

¹/₂ cup heavy cream

warm crusty bread, to serve

1 Finely chop 1 onion. Melt the butter in a large saucepan and add the onion, carrots, rutabaga, turnip, parsnip, and potatoes. Cover and cook gently for about 10 minutes, without browning, stirring occasionally.

2 Add the stock, and season to taste with the nutmeg, salt, and pepper. Cover and bring to a boil, then reduce the heat and simmer gently for 15–20 minutes, or until the vegetables are tender. Remove from the heat and let cool for 30 minutes.

3 Heat the oil in a large heavy skillet. Add the onions and cook over medium heat for about 2–3 minutes, stirring frequently, until golden brown. Remove the onions with a slotted spoon and drain well on paper towels. As they cool, they will turn crispy.

4 Pour the cooled soup into a food processor or blender, and process to form a smooth puree. Return to the cleaned pan, adjust the seasoning, then stir in the cream. Gently reheat, and top with the crispy onions. Serve immediately with chunks of bread.

HELPFUL HINT

For a lower-fat version of this delicious soup, add milk (skim milk if desired) rather than cream when reheating.

1

3

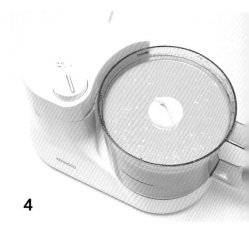

4

Potato, Leek & Rosemary Soup

INGREDIENTS

Serves 4

4 tbsp. butter
1 lb. leeks, trimmed and finely sliced
4 cups peeled and coarsely
 chopped potatoes
$3^3/_4$ cups vegetable stock
4 fresh rosemary sprigs
2 cups whole milk
2 tbsp. freshly chopped parsley
2 tbsp. crème fraîche
salt and freshly ground black pepper
whole-wheat rolls, to serve

TASTY TIP

This rosemary-scented version of vichyssoise is equally delicious served cold. Let the soup cool before covering, then chill in the refrigerator for at least 2 hours. The soup will thicken as it chills, so you may need to thin it to the desired consistency with more milk or stock, and season before serving. It is important to use fresh rosemary rather than dried for this recipe. If unavailable, use 2 bay leaves, or add a bruised, fresh lemongrass stalk.

1 Melt the butter in a large saucepan, add the leeks, and cook gently for 5 minutes, stirring frequently. Remove 1 tablespoon of the cooked leeks and set aside for garnishing.

2 Add the potatoes, vegetable stock, rosemary sprigs, and milk. Bring to a boil, then reduce the heat, cover, and simmer gently for 20–25 minutes, or until the vegetables are tender.

3 Cool for 10 minutes. Discard the rosemary, then pour into a food processor or blender, and blend well to form a smooth-textured soup.

4 Return the soup to the cleaned saucepan and stir in the chopped parsley and crème fraîche. Season to taste with salt and pepper. If the soup is too thick, stir in a little more milk or water. Reheat gently, without boiling, then ladle into warm soup bowls. Garnish the soup with the set-aside leeks and serve immediately with whole-wheat rolls.

Cream of Spinach Soup

INGREDIENTS

Serves 6–8

1 large onion, peeled and chopped

5 large garlic cloves, peeled
  and chopped

2 medium potatoes, peeled
  and chopped

1 tsp. salt

1 lb. spinach, washed and large
  stems removed

4 tbsp. butter

3 tbsp. all-purpose flour

3¼ cups milk

½ tsp. freshly grated nutmeg

freshly ground black pepper

6–8 tbsp. crème fraîche or
  sour cream

warm foccacia bread, to serve

HELPFUL HINT

When choosing spinach, always look for fresh, crisp, dark-green leaves. Store in a cool place until needed and use within 1–2 days of buying. To prepare, wash several times to remove any dirt or grit, and shake off as much excess water as possible.

1 Place the onion, garlic, and potatoes in a large saucepan and cover with 3¼ cups cold water. Add half the salt and bring to a boil. Cover and simmer for 15–20 minutes, or until the potatoes are tender. Remove from the heat and add the spinach. Cover and set aside for 10 minutes.

2 Slowly melt the butter in another saucepan, add the flour, and cook over low heat for about 2 minutes. Remove the saucepan from the heat and add the milk a little at a time, stirring continuously. Return to the heat and cook, stirring continuously for 5–8 minutes, or until the sauce is smooth and slightly thickened. Add the freshly grated nutmeg or pepper to taste.

3 Blend the cooled potato and spinach mixture in a food processor or blender to a smooth puree, then return to the saucepan and gradually stir in the white sauce. Season to taste with salt and pepper, and gently reheat, taking care not to let the soup boil. Ladle into soup bowls and top with spoonfuls of crème fraîche or sour cream. Serve immediately with warm foccacia bread.

Bacon & Split Pea Soup

INGREDIENTS

Serves 4

¹/₃ cup dried split peas
2 tbsp. butter
1 garlic clove, peeled and
  finely chopped
1 medium onion, peeled and
  thinly sliced
1 cup long-grain rice
2 tbsp. tomato paste
5 cups vegetable or chicken stock
1 cup peeled and finely diced carrots
4 slices bacon, finely chopped
salt and freshly ground black pepper
2 tbsp. freshly chopped parsley
4 tbsp. light cream
warm, crusty garlic bread, to serve

1 Cover the dried split peas with plenty of cold water, cover loosely, and let soak for a minimum of 12 hours, preferably overnight.

2 Melt the butter in a heavy saucepan, add the garlic and onion, and cook for 2–3 minutes, without browning. Add the rice, drained split peas, and tomato paste, and cook for 2–3 minutes, stirring constantly to prevent sticking. Add the stock, bring to a boil, then reduce the heat and simmer for 20–25 minutes, or until the rice and peas are tender. Remove from the heat and let cool.

3 Blend about three-quarters of the soup in a food processor, or blender, to form a smooth puree. Pour this into the remaining soup in the saucepan. Add the carrots and cook for an additional 10–12 minutes, or until the carrots are tender.

4 Meanwhile, place the bacon in a nonstick skillet, and cook over gentle heat until the bacon is crisp. Remove and drain on paper towels.

5 Season the soup with salt and pepper to taste, then stir in the parsley and cream. Reheat for 2–3 minutes, then ladle into soup bowls. Sprinkle with the bacon and serve immediately with warm garlic bread.

2

3

3

Squash & Smoked Haddock Soup

INGREDIENTS

Serves 4–6

2 tbsp. olive oil

1 medium onion, peeled and chopped

2 garlic cloves, peeled and chopped

3 celery stalks, trimmed and chopped

1½ lb. squash, peeled, seeded, and
   cut into chunks

2⅔ cups peeled and coarsely
   diced potatoes

3¼ cups chicken stock, heated

½ cup dry sherry

½ lb. smoked haddock fillet

⅔ cup milk

freshly ground black pepper

2 tbsp. freshly chopped parsley

1 Heat the oil in a large heavy saucepan and gently cook the onion, garlic, and celery for about 10 minutes. This will release the sweetness but not brown the vegetables. Add the squash and potatoes to the saucepan and stir to coat the vegetables with the oil.

2 Gradually add the stock and bring to a boil. Cover, then reduce the heat and simmer for 25 minutes, stirring occasionally. Stir in the dry sherry, then remove the saucepan from the heat and let cool for 5–10 minutes.

3 Blend the mixture in a food processor, or blender, to form a chunky puree, and return to the cleaned saucepan.

4 Meanwhile, place the fish in a skillet. Pour in the milk with 3 tablespoons water and bring almost to the boiling point. Reduce the heat, cover, and simmer for 6 minutes, or until the fish is cooked and flakes easily. Remove from the heat and, using a slotted spoon, remove the fish from the liquid, setting aside both liquid and fish.

5 Discard the skin and any bones from the fish and flake into pieces. Stir the fish liquid into the soup, together with the flaked fish. Season with freshly ground black pepper, stir in the parsley, and serve immediately.

TASTY TIP

Use smoked salmon if haddock is not easily available. Butternut squash works nicely in this recipe.

1

4

5

Clear Chicken & Mushroom Soup

INGREDIENTS

Serves 4

2 large chicken legs, about
  1 lb. total weight
1 tbsp. peanut oil
1 tsp. sesame oil
1 onion, peeled and very thinly sliced
1 in. piece fresh ginger, peeled and
  very finely chopped
5 cups clear chicken stock
1 lemongrass stalk, bruised
1/3 cup long-grain rice
1 cup wiped and finely sliced
  baby mushrooms
4 scallions, trimmed, cut into
  2-in. pieces, and shredded
1 tbsp. dark soy sauce
4 tbsp. dry sherry
salt and freshly ground black pepper

FOOD FACT

When using sesame oil for stir-frying, as in this recipe, it is important to use it with another cooking oil, like sunflower oil—otherwise it will burn.

1 Skin the chicken legs and remove any fat. Cut each in half to make 2 thigh and 2 drumstick portions, and set aside. Heat the peanut and sesame oils in a large saucepan. Add the sliced onion and cook gently for 10 minutes, or until soft but not beginning to brown.

2 Add the chopped ginger to the saucepan, and cook for about 30 seconds, stirring constantly to prevent it from sticking, then pour in the stock. Add the chicken and the lemongrass, cover, and simmer gently for 15 minutes. Stir in the rice and cook for an additional 15 minutes, or until the chicken is cooked.

3 Remove the chicken from the saucepan and leave until cool enough to handle. Finely shred the flesh, then return to the saucepan with the mushrooms, scallions, soy sauce, and sherry. Simmer for 5 minutes, or until the rice and mushrooms are tender. Remove the lemongrass.

4 Season the soup to taste with salt and pepper. Ladle into warmed serving bowls, making sure each has an equal amount of shredded chicken and vegetables, and serve immediately.

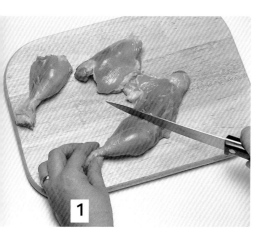

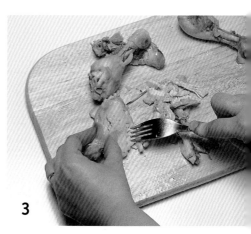

Wonton Noodle Soup

INGREDIENTS

Serves 4

4 dried shiitake mushrooms, wiped

³/₄ cup peeled and finely chopped
  shrimp

¹/₄ lb. ground pork

4 water chestnuts, finely chopped

4 scallions, trimmed and finely sliced

1 large egg white

salt and freshly ground black pepper

1¹/₂ tsp. cornstarch

1 package fresh wonton wrappers

5 cups chicken stock

³/₄-in. piece fresh ginger, peeled and
  sliced

3 oz. thin egg noodles

1 cup shredded bok choy

1 Place the mushrooms in a bowl, cover with warm water, and let soak for 1 hour. Drain, remove, and discard the stalks, and finely chop the mushrooms. Return to the bowl with the shrimp, pork, water chestnuts, 2 of the scallions, and the egg white. Season to taste with salt and pepper. Mix well.

2 Mix the cornstarch with 1 tablespoon cold water to make a paste. Place a wonton wrapper on a board, and brush the edges with the paste. Drop a little less than 1 teaspoon of the pork mixture in the center, then fold in half to make a triangle, pressing the edges together. Bring the 2 outer corners together, pressing together with a little more paste. Continue until all the pork mixture is used up; you should have 16–20 wontons.

3 Pour the stock into a large, wide saucepan, add the ginger slices, and bring to a boil. Add the wontons, reduce the heat, and simmer for about 5 minutes. Add the noodles and cook for 1 minute. Stir in the bok choy and cook for an additional 2 minutes, or until the noodles and bok choy are tender, and the wontons have floated to the surface and are cooked through.

4 Ladle the soup into warmed bowls, discarding the ginger. Sprinkle with the remaining sliced scallions, and serve immediately.

FOOD FACT

Wonton wrappers are thin sheets, about 4 in. square, of noodle dough made from eggs and flour. Buy them fresh or frozen from larger supermarkets and Asian markets.

1

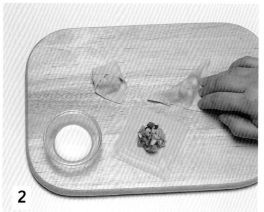

2

3

Thai Shellfish Soup

INGREDIENTS

Serves 4–6

³/₄ lb. shrimp

³/₄ lb. firm white fish, such
  as monkfish

6 oz. small squid

1 tbsp. lime juice

1 lb. live mussels

2 cups coconut milk

1 tbsp. peanut oil

2 tbsp. Thai red curry paste

1 lemongrass stalk, bruised

3 kaffir lime leaves, finely shredded

2 tbsp. Thai fish sauce

salt and freshly ground black pepper

fresh cilantro, to garnish

1 Peel the shrimp. Using a sharp knife, remove the black vein along the back of the shrimp. Pat dry with paper towels and set aside.

2 Skin the fish, pat dry, and cut into 1-inch chunks. Place in a bowl with the shrimp and the squid. Sprinkle with the lime juice and set aside.

3 Scrub the mussels, removing their beards and any barnacles. Discard any mussels that are open, damaged, or do not close when tapped. Place in a large saucepan and add ²/₃ cup coconut milk.

4 Cover, bring to a boil, then reduce the heat and simmer for 5 minutes, or until the mussels open, shaking the saucepan occasionally. Lift out the mussels, discarding any unopened ones, strain the liquid through a cheesecloth-lined strainer, and set aside.

5 Rinse and dry the saucepan. Heat the peanut oil, add the curry paste, and cook for 1 minute, stirring all the time. Add the lemongrass, lime leaves, fish sauce, the strained mussel liquid, and the remaining coconut milk. Bring the contents of the saucepan to a very gentle simmer.

6 Add the fish mixture to the saucepan, and simmer for 2–3 minutes, or until just cooked. Stir in the mussels, with or without their shells, as preferred. Season to taste with salt and pepper, then garnish with cilantro. Ladle into warmed bowls and serve immediately.

FOOD FACT

Squeezing lime juice on top of seafood improves its texture—the acid in the juice firms up the flesh.

2

3

4

Thai Hot & Sour Shrimp Soup

INGREDIENTS

Serves 6

1½ lb. large shrimp

2 tbsp. vegetable oil

3–4 lemongrass stalks, coarsely
   chopped and outer leaves discarded

1-in. piece fresh ginger, peeled and
   finely chopped

2–3 garlic cloves, peeled and crushed

small bunch fresh cilantro, leaves
   stripped and set aside, stems
   finely chopped

½ tsp. freshly ground black pepper

1–2 small red chiles, seeded and
   thinly sliced

1–2 small green chiles, seeded and
   thinly sliced

6 kaffir lime leaves, thinly shredded

4 scallions, trimmed and
   diagonally sliced

1–2 tbsp. Thai fish sauce

1–2 tbsp. freshly squeezed lime juice

1 Remove the heads from the shrimp by twisting away from the body, and set aside. Peel the shrimp, leaving the tails on, and set aside the shells with the heads. Using a sharp knife, remove the black vein from the back of the shrimp. Rinse and dry the shrimp and set aside. Rinse and dry the heads and shells.

2 Heat a wok, add the oil, and, when hot, add the shrimp heads and shells, the lemongrass, ginger, garlic, cilantro stems, and black pepper, and stir-fry for 2–3 minutes, or until the shrimp heads and shells turn pink and all the ingredients are colored.

3 Carefully add 6 cups water to the wok and return to a boil, skimming off any scum that rises to the surface. Simmer over medium heat for 10 minutes, or until slightly reduced. Strain through a fine strainer and return the clear shrimp stock to the wok.

4 Bring the stock back to a boil and add the shrimp, chiles, lime leaves, and scallions, and simmer for 3 minutes, or until the shrimp turn pink. Season with the fish sauce and lime juice. Spoon into heated soup bowls, dividing the shrimp evenly, and sprinkle a few cilantro leaves over the surface.

FOOD FACT

Thai fish sauce, made from fermented anchovies, has a sour, salty, fishy flavor.

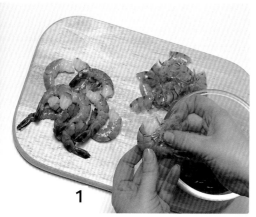
1

2

4

Creamy Caribbean Chicken & Coconut Soup

INGREDIENTS

Serves 4

6–8 scallions

2 garlic cloves

1 red chile

2 cups shredded or diced
  cooked chicken

2 tbsp. vegetable oil

1 tsp. turmeric

1 cup coconut milk

3 cups chicken stock

½ cup small soup pasta or spaghetti,
  broken into small pieces

½ lemon, sliced

salt and freshly ground black pepper

1–2 tbsp. freshly chopped cilantro

fresh cilantro sprigs, to garnish

HELPFUL HINT

Be careful handling chiles. Either wear rubber gloves or scrub your hands with plenty of soap and water, and avoid touching your eyes and any other sensitive areas.

1 Trim the scallions and slice thinly; peel the garlic and chop finely. Cut off the top from the chile, slit down the side and remove the seeds and membrane, then chop finely and set aside.

2 Remove and discard any skin or bones from the cooked chicken and shred, using two forks, and set aside.

3 Heat a large wok, add the oil and, when hot, add the scallions, garlic, and chile, and stir-fry for 2 minutes, or until the scallions have softened. Stir in the turmeric and cook for 1 minute.

4 Blend the coconut milk with the chicken stock until smooth, then pour into the wok. Add the pasta or spaghetti with the lemon slices, and bring to a boil.

5 Reduce the heat and simmer, half covered, for 10–12 minutes, or until the pasta is tender; stir occasionally.

6 Remove the lemon slices from the wok and add the chicken. Season to taste with salt and pepper, and simmer for 2–3 minutes, or until the chicken is heated through.

7 Stir in the chopped cilantro and ladle into heated bowls. Garnish with sprigs of fresh cilantro and serve immediately.

2

3

6

Corn & Crab Soup

INGREDIENTS

Serves 4

1 lb. fresh corn on the cob

5 cups chicken stock

2–3 scallions, trimmed and
finely chopped

½-in. piece fresh ginger, peeled and
finely chopped

1 tbsp. Chinese rice wine

2–3 tsp. soy sauce

1 tsp. light brown sugar

salt and freshly ground black pepper

2 tsp. cornstarch

½ lb. white crabmeat, fresh
or canned

1 large egg white

1 tsp. sesame oil

1–2 tbsp. freshly chopped cilantro

1 Wash and dry the corncobs. Using a sharp knife and holding the corncobs at an angle to the cutting board, cut down along the cobs to remove the kernels, then scrape the cobs to remove any excess milky residue. Put the kernels and the milky residue into a large wok.

2 Add the chicken stock to the wok and place over high heat. Bring to a boil, stirring and pressing some of the kernels against the side of the wok to squeeze out the starch to help thicken the soup. Simmer for 15 minutes, stirring occasionally.

3 Add the scallions, ginger, Chinese rice wine, soy sauce, and brown sugar to the wok, and season to taste with salt and pepper. Simmer for an additional 5 minutes, stirring occasionally.

4 Blend the cornstarch with 1 tablespoon cold water to form a smooth paste, and mix into the soup. Return to a boil, then reduce the heat to medium and simmer until thickened.

5 Add the crabmeat, stirring until blended. Beat the egg white with the sesame oil and stir into the soup in a slow, steady stream, stirring constantly. Stir in the chopped cilantro and serve immediately.

TASTY TIP

If you cannot obtain Chinese rice wine, dry sherry makes a very good substitute.

1

2

4

Hot & Sour Soup

INGREDIENTS

Serves 4–6

¼ cup dried shiitake mushrooms

2 tbsp. peanut oil

1 carrot, peeled and cut into
    julienne strips

1 cup wiped and thinly sliced crimini
    or brown mushrooms

2 garlic cloves, peeled and
    finely chopped

½ tsp. dried crushed chiles

5 cups chicken stock

1 cup shredded boneless cooked
    chicken or pork

½ cup thinly sliced fresh tofu
    (optional)

2–3 scallions, trimmed and finely
    sliced diagonally

1–2 tsp. sugar

3 tbsp. vinegar

2 tbsp. soy sauce

salt and freshly ground black pepper

1 tbsp. cornstarch

1 extra-large egg

2 tsp. sesame oil

2 tbsp. freshly chopped cilantro

1 Place the dried shiitake mushrooms in a small bowl, and add enough almost-boiling water to cover. Leave for 20 minutes to soften, then gently lift out and squeeze out the liquid. (Lifting out the mushrooms leaves any sand and grit behind.) Discard the stems and thinly slice the caps, and set aside.

2 Heat a large wok, add the oil, and when hot, add the carrot strips and stir-fry for 2–3 minutes, or until beginning to soften. Add the crimini mushrooms and stir-fry for 2–3 minutes, or until golden, then stir in the garlic and chiles.

3 Add the chicken stock to the vegetables and bring to a boil, skimming any foam that rises to the surface. Add the shredded chicken or pork, tofu (if using), scallions, sugar, vinegar, soy sauce, and the shiitake mushrooms. Simmer for 5 minutes, stirring occasionally. Season to taste with salt and pepper.

4 Blend the cornstarch with 1 tablespoon of cold water to form a smooth paste, and beat into the soup. Return to a boil, reduce the heat, and simmer over medium heat until thickened.

5 Beat the egg with the sesame oil and slowly add to the soup in a slow, steady stream, stirring constantly. Stir in the chopped cilantro and serve the soup immediately.

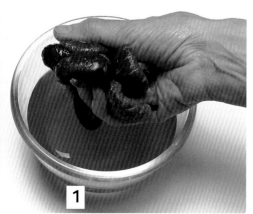

Chinese Cabbage & Mushroom Soup

INGREDIENTS

Serves 4–6

1 lb. Chinese cabbage

¼ cup dried shiitake mushrooms

1 tbsp. vegetable oil

⅓ cup bacon, diced

1-in. piece fresh ginger, peeled and
   finely chopped

1½ cups thinly sliced crimini or
   brown mushrooms

5 cups chicken stock

4–6 scallions, trimmed and cut into
   short lengths

2 tbsp. dry sherry or Chinese
   rice wine

salt and freshly ground black pepper

sesame oil, for drizzling

1 Trim the stem ends of the Chinese cabbage and cut in half lengthwise. Remove the triangular core, then cut into 1-inch slices and set aside.

2 Place the dried shiitake mushrooms in a bowl and add enough almost-boiling water to cover. Let stand for 20 minutes to soften, then gently lift out and squeeze out the liquid. Discard the stems and thinly slice the caps, and set aside. Strain the liquid through a cheesecloth-lined strainer and set aside.

3 Heat a wok over medium-high heat, add the oil and, when hot, add the bacon. Stir-fry for 3–4 minutes, or until crisp and golden, stirring frequently. Add the ginger and crimini mushrooms, and stir-fry for an additional 2–3 minutes.

4 Add the chicken stock and bring to a boil, skimming off any fat and scum that rises to the surface. Add the scallions, sherry or rice wine, Chinese cabbage, and sliced Chinese mushrooms, and season to taste with salt and pepper. Pour in the reserved soaking liquid and reduce the heat to the lowest possible setting.

5 Simmer gently, covered, until all the vegetables are very tender; this will take about 10 minutes. Add a little water if the liquid has reduced too much. Spoon into soup bowls and drizzle with a little sesame oil. Serve immediately.

TASTY TIP

If Chinese cabbage is not available, use bok choy.

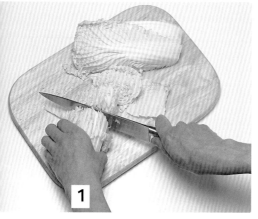

Vietnamese Beef & Rice Noodle Soup

INGREDIENTS

Serves 4–6

For the beef stock:
2 lb. meaty beef bones
1 large onion, peeled and quartered
2 carrots, peeled and cut into chunks
2 celery stalks, trimmed and sliced
1 leek, washed and sliced into chunks
2 garlic cloves, unpeeled and
   lightly crushed
3 whole star anise
1 tsp. black peppercorns

For the soup:
2½ cups dried rice stick noodles
4–6 scallions, trimmed and
   sliced diagonally
1 red chile, seeded and
   sliced diagonally
1 small bunch fresh cilantro
1 small bunch fresh mint
¾ lb. beef tenderloin,
   very thinly sliced
salt and freshly ground black pepper

1 Place all the ingredients for the beef stock into a large stockpot or saucepan and cover with cold water. Bring to a boil and skim off any scum that rises to the surface. Reduce the heat and simmer gently, partially covered, for 2–3 hours, skimming occasionally.

2 Strain into a large bowl and let cool, then skim off the fat. Chill in the refrigerator, and when cold, remove any fat from the surface. Pour 6 cups of the stock into a large wok and set aside.

3 Cover the noodles with warm water and leave for 3 minutes, or until just softened. Drain, then cut into 4-inch lengths.

4 Arrange the scallions and chile on a serving platter or large serving plate. Strip the leaves from the cilantro and mint, and then arrange them in piles on the plate.

5 Bring the stock in the wok to a boil over high heat. Add the noodles and simmer for about 2 minutes, or until tender. Add the beef strips and simmer for about 1 minute. Season to taste with salt and pepper.

6 Ladle the soup with the noodles and beef strips into individual soup bowls, and serve immediately with the plate of condiments handed around separately.

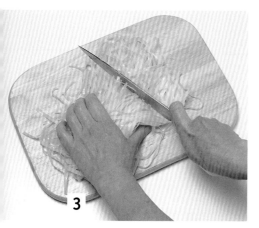
3

4

5

Laksa Malayan Rice Noodle Soup

INGREDIENTS

Serves 4–6

2½ lb. corn-fed,
  free-range chicken
1 tsp. black peppercorns
1 tbsp. vegetable oil
1 large onion, peeled and thinly sliced
2 garlic cloves, peeled and
  finely chopped
1-in. piece fresh ginger, peeled and
  thinly sliced
1 tsp. ground coriander
2 red chiles, seeded and
  diagonally sliced
1–2 tsp. hot curry paste
1½ cups coconut milk
1 lb. large shrimp, peeled
  and deveined
½ small head Chinese cabbage,
  thinly shredded
1 tsp. sugar
2 scallions, trimmed and thinly sliced
¾ cup bean sprouts
3½ cups rice noodles or rice sticks,
  soaked according to
  package instructions
fresh mint leaves, to garnish

1. Put the chicken in a large saucepan with the peppercorns, and cover with cold water. Bring to a boil, skimming off any scum that rises to the surface. Reduce the heat and simmer, partially covered, for about 1 hour. Remove the chicken and cool. Skim any fat from the stock and strain through a cheesecloth-lined strainer, and set aside. Remove the meat from the carcass, shred, and set aside

2. Heat a large wok, add the vegetable oil, and, when hot, add the onion and stir-fry for 2 minutes, or until they begin to brown. Stir in the garlic, ginger, coriander, chiles, and curry paste, and stir-fry for an additional 2 minutes.

3. Pour in the set-aside stock (you need at least 5 cups) and simmer gently, partially covered, for 10 minutes, or until slightly reduced.

4. Add the coconut milk, shrimp, Chinese cabbage, sugar, scallions, and bean sprouts, and simmer for 3 minutes, stirring occasionally. Add the shredded chicken and cook for an additional 2 minutes.

5. Drain the noodles and divide among 4–6 soup bowls. Ladle the hot stock and vegetables over the noodles, making sure each serving has some shrimp and chicken. Garnish each bowl with fresh mint leaves and serve immediately.

White Bean Soup with Parmesan Croutons

INGREDIENTS

Serves 4

3 thick slices white bread, cut into
  ½-in. cubes
3 tbsp. peanut oil
2 tbsp. finely grated Parmesan cheese
1 tbsp. light olive oil
1 large onion, peeled and
  finely chopped
½ cup diced bacon
1 tbsp. fresh thyme leaves
2 14-oz. cans canellini beans, drained
3 cups chicken stock
salt and freshly ground black pepper
1 tbsp. prepared pesto sauce
½ cup diced pepperoni sausage
1 tbsp. fresh lemon juice
1 tbsp. freshly torn basil

1 Preheat the oven to 400°F. Place the cubes of bread in a bowl and pour over the peanut oil. Stir to coat the bread, then sprinkle over the Parmesan cheese. Place on a lightly greased baking sheet, and cook in the preheated oven for 10 minutes, or until crisp and golden brown.

2 Heat the olive oil in a large saucepan and cook the onion for 4–5 minutes until softened. Add the bacon and thyme, and cook for an additional 3 minutes. Stir in the beans, stock, and black pepper, then simmer gently for 5 minutes.

3 Place half the bean mixture and liquid into a food processor, and blend until smooth.

4 Return the puree to the saucepan. Stir in the pesto sauce, pepperoni sausage, and lemon juice. Season to taste with salt and pepper.

5 Return the soup to the heat, and cook for an additional 2–3 minutes until piping hot. Place some of the beans in each serving bowl and add a ladleful of soup. Garnish with torn basil, and sprinkle croutons over the top.

Rice Soup with Potato Sticks

INGREDIENTS

Serves 4

¾ cup (1½ sticks) butter

1 tsp. olive oil

1 large onion, peeled and
  finely chopped

4 slices prosciutto, chopped

½ cup risotto rice

5 cups chicken stock

3 cups frozen peas

salt and freshly ground black pepper

1 large egg

1 cup self-rising flour

¾ cup mashed potato

1 tbsp. milk

1 tbsp. poppy seeds

1 tbsp. finely grated Parmesan cheese

1 tbsp. freshly chopped parsley

TASTY TIP

These potato sticks also make a delicious snack with drinks. Try sprinkling them with sesame seeds or shredded cheese, and let cool before serving.

1 Preheat the oven to 375° F. Heat 2 tbsp. of the butter and the olive oil in a large, heavy saucepan and cook the onion for 4–5 minutes until softened, then add the prosciutto and cook for about 1 minute. Stir in the rice, stock, and peas. Season to taste with salt and pepper, and simmer for 10–15 minutes, or until the rice is tender.

2 Beat the egg and ½ cup (1 stick) of the butter together until smooth, then beat in the flour, a pinch of salt, and the mashed potato. Form a soft, pliable dough, adding a little flour if necessary.

3 Roll the dough out on a lightly floured surface into a rectangle about ½ inch thick, and cut into 12 thin, long sticks. Brush with milk and sprinkle with the poppy seeds. Place the sticks on a lightly greased baking sheet and cook in the preheated oven for 15 minutes until golden.

4 When the rice is cooked, stir the remaining butter and Parmesan cheese into the soup and sprinkle with chopped parsley. Serve immediately with the warm potato sticks.

1

2

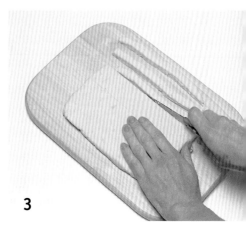

3

Arugula & Potato Soup with Garlic Croutons

INGREDIENTS

Serves 4

1½ lb. baby new potatoes

5 cups chicken or
  vegetable stock

1¼ cups arugula

4 slices thick white bread

½ stick unsalted butter

1 tsp. peanut oil

2–4 garlic cloves, peeled
  and chopped

4 slices stale ciabatta bread, with the
  crusts removed

¼ cup olive oil

salt and freshly ground black pepper

2 tbsp. shredded Parmesan cheese

HELPFUL HINT

Arugula is now widely available in bags from most large grocery stores. If, however, you cannot find it, replace it with an equal quantity of watercress or baby spinach leaves.

1 Place the potatoes in a large saucepan, cover with the stock, and simmer gently for 10 minutes. Add the arugula and simmer for an additional 5–10 minutes, or until the potatoes are soft and the arugula has wilted.

2 Meanwhile, make the croutons. Cut the bread slices into small cubes and set aside. Heat the butter and peanut oil in a small skillet and cook the garlic for 1 minute, stirring well. Remove the garlic, then add the bread cubes to the butter and oil mixture in the skillet and sauté, stirring continuously, until they are golden brown. Drain the croutons on absorbent paper towels and set aside.

3 Cut the slices of ciabatta bread into small pieces and stir into soup. Cover the saucepan and let stand for 10 minutes, or until the bread has absorbed a lot of the liquid.

4 Stir in the olive oil, season to taste with salt and pepper, and serve at once with a few of the garlic croutons sprinkled over top and a little grated Parmesan cheese.

Classic Minestrone

INGREDIENTS

Serves 6–8

2 tbsp. butter

3 tbsp. olive oil

3 slices bacon

1 large onion, peeled

1 garlic clove, peeled

1 celery stalk, trimmed

2 carrots, peeled

14 oz. canned chopped tomatoes

5 cups chicken stock

1½ cups finely shredded
  green cabbage

½ cup trimmed and halved fine
  green beans

3 tbsp. frozen peas

2 oz. spaghetti, broken into
  short pieces (¾ cup)

salt and freshly ground black pepper

Parmesan cheese, to garnish

crusty bread, to serve

1 Heat the butter and olive oil together in a large saucepan. Chop the bacon and add to the saucepan. Cook for 3–4 minutes, then remove with a slotted spoon and set aside.

2 Finely chop the onion, garlic, celery, and carrots, and add to the saucepan, one ingredient at a time, stirring well after each addition. Cover and cook gently for 8–10 minutes until vegetables soften.

3 Add the chopped tomatoes, with their juice and the stock, bring to a boil, then cover the saucepan with a lid, reduce the heat, and simmer gently for about 20 minutes.

4 Stir in the cabbage, beans, peas, and spaghetti. Cover and simmer for an additional 20 minutes, or until all the ingredients are tender. Season to taste with salt and pepper.

5 Return the cooked bacon to the saucepan and bring the soup to a boil. Serve the soup immediately with Parmesan cheese shavings sprinkled on the top and plenty of crusty bread.

Cream of Pumpkin Soup

INGREDIENTS

Serves 4

2 lb. pumpkin flesh (after peeling and
  discarding the seeds)

¼ cup olive oil

1 large onion, peeled

1 leek, trimmed

1 carrot, peeled

2 celery stalks

4 garlic cloves, peeled
  and crushed

salt and freshly ground black pepper

¼ tsp. freshly grated nutmeg

⅔ cup light cream

¼ tsp. cayenne pepper

warm herb bread, to serve

TASTY TIP

If you cannot find pumpkin, try
replacing it with squash. Butternut
or acorn squash would both make
suitable substitutes. However,
avoid spaghetti squash, which
gets too soft when cooked.

1 Cut the peeled and seeded pumpkin flesh into 1-inch cubes. Heat
the olive oil in a large saucepan and cook the pumpkin for 2–3
minutes, coating it completely with oil. Chop the onion and leek
finely, and dice the carrot and celery stalks.

2 Add the vegetables to the saucepan with the garlic and cook,
stirring, for 5 minutes, or until they have begun to soften. Cover
the vegetables with 6 cups water and bring to a boil. Season with
plenty of salt, pepper, and the grated nutmeg, then reduce the heat,
cover, and simmer for 15–20 minutes or until all of the vegetables
are tender.

3 When the vegetables are tender, remove from the heat, cool slightly,
then pour into a food processor or blender. Blend to form a smooth
paste, then pass through a strainer into a clean saucepan.

4 Adjust the seasoning to taste and add all but 2 tablespoons of the
cream and enough water to obtain the correct consistency. Bring
the soup to boiling point, add the cayenne pepper, and serve
immediately swirled with the remaining cream and warm
herb bread.

Lettuce Soup

INGREDIENTS

Serves 4

2 heads iceberg lettuce, quartered,
   with tough core removed
1 tbsp. olive oil
4 tbsp. butter
½ cup scallions, trimmed
   and chopped
1 tbsp. freshly chopped parsley
1 tbsp. all-purpose flour
2½ cups chicken stock
salt and freshly ground black pepper
⅔ cup light cream
¼ tsp. cayenne pepper, or to taste
thick slices stale ciabatta bread
parsley sprigs, to garnish

1 Bring a large saucepan of water to the boil and blanch the lettuce leaves for 3 minutes. Drain and dry thoroughly on absorbent paper towels. Then shred with a sharp knife.

2 Heat the olive oil and butter in a clean saucepan and add the lettuce, scallions, and parsley, and cook together for 3–4 minutes, or until very soft.

3 Stir in the flour and cook for 1 minute, then gradually pour in the stock, stirring throughout. Bring to a boil and season to taste with salt and pepper. Reduce the heat, cover, and simmer gently for 10–15 minutes, or until soft.

4 Let the soup cool slightly, then either strain or puree in a blender. Alternatively, leave the soup chunky. Stir in the cream, add more seasoning to taste, if liked, then add the cayenne pepper.

5 Arrange the slices of ciabatta bread in a large soup dish or in individual bowls and pour the soup over the bread. Garnish with sprigs of parsley and serve immediately.

HELPFUL HINT

Do not prepare the lettuce too far in advance. Iceberg lettuce has a tendency to discolor when sliced, which may discolor the soup.

2

3

4

Pasta & Bean Soup

INGREDIENTS

Serves 4–6

3 tbsp. olive oil

2 celery stalks, trimmed and
  finely chopped

3¹/₂ oz. prosciutto or speck, cut
  in pieces (³/₄ cup)

1 red chile, seeded and
  finely chopped

2 large potatoes, peeled and cut into
  1-in. cubes

2 garlic cloves, peeled and
  finely chopped

3 ripe plum tomatoes, skinned
  and chopped

14 oz. canned cranberry beans,
  drained and rinsed

4 cups chicken or vegetable stock

1 cup pasta shapes

large handful basil leaves, torn

salt and freshly ground black pepper

freshly shredded basil leaves,
  to garnish

crusty bread, to serve

1 Heat the olive oil in a heavy pan. Add the celery and prosciutto, and cook gently for 6–8 minutes, or until softened. Add the chopped chile and potato cubes and cook for an additional 10 minutes.

2 Add the garlic to the chile and potato mixture, and cook for 1 minute. Add the chopped tomatoes and simmer for 5 minutes. Stir in two-thirds of the beans, then pour in the chicken or vegetable stock and bring to a boil.

3 Add the pasta shapes to the soup stock and return it to simmering point. Cook the pasta for about 10 minutes, or until al dente.

4 Meanwhile, place the remaining beans in a food processor or blender and blend with enough of the soup stock to make a smooth, thin puree.

5 When the pasta is cooked, stir in the pureed beans with the torn basil. Season the soup to taste with salt and pepper. Ladle into serving bowls. Garnish with shredded basil and serve immediately with plenty of crusty bread.

Appetizers

Get ready to impress friends and family with these tasty, tempting hors d'oeuvres. Prepare a meat, fish, or vegetable dish to cater to any preference. Whether you desire a quick and simple recipe or a more elaborate, sophisticated one, you will find everything you're looking for in our wide variety of appetizers.

Mushroom & Red Wine Pâté

INGREDIENTS

Serves 4

3 large slices white bread,
  crusts removed
2 tsp. oil
1 small onion, peeled and
  finely chopped
1 garlic clove, peeled
  and crushed
$3^3/_4$ cups wiped and finely chopped
  baby mushrooms
$^2/_3$ cup red wine
$^1/_2$ tsp. dried mixed herbs
1 tbsp. freshly chopped parsley
salt and freshly ground black pepper
2 tbsp. low-fat cream cheese

To serve:
finely chopped cucumber
finely chopped tomato

TASTY TIP

This pâté is also delicious served as a bruschetta topping. Toast slices of ciabatta, generously spread the pâté on top, and garnish with a little arugula.

1   Preheat the oven to 350°F. Cut the bread in half diagonally. Place the bread triangles on a baking sheet and cook for 10 minutes.

2   Remove from the oven and split each bread triangle in half to make 12 triangles, and return to the oven until golden and crisp. Let cool on a wire rack.

3   Heat the oil in a saucepan and gently cook the onion and garlic until transparent.

4   Add the mushrooms and cook, stirring for 3–4 minutes, or until the mushroom juices start to run.

5   Stir the wine and herbs into the mushroom mixture and bring to a boil. Reduce the heat and simmer uncovered until all the liquid is absorbed.

6   Remove from the heat and season to taste with salt and pepper. Let cool.

7   When cold, beat in the cream cheese and season lightly. Place in a small, clean bowl and chill in the refrigerator until needed. Serve the toast triangles with the cucumber and tomato.

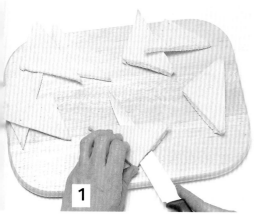

1

5

7

Thai Fish Cakes

INGREDIENTS

Serves 4

1 red chile, seeded and coarsely chopped
4 tbsp. coarsely chopped fresh cilantro
1 garlic clove, peeled and crushed
2 scallions, trimmed and
   coarsely chopped
1 lemongrass, outer leaves discarded
   and coarsely chopped
3 oz. shrimp, thawed if frozen
10 oz. cod fillet, skinned, pin bones
   removed, and cubed
salt and freshly ground black pepper
sweet chile dipping sauce, to serve

1 Preheat the oven to 375°F. Place the chile, cilantro, garlic, scallions, and lemongrass in a food processor and blend together.

2 Pat the shrimp and cod dry with paper towels.

3 Add to the food processor and blend until the mixture is coarsely chopped.

4 Season to taste with salt and pepper, and blend to mix.

5 Dampen your hands, then shape heaping tablespoons of the mixture into 12 little patties. Place the patties on a lightly greased baking pan.

6 Cook in the preheated oven for 12–15 minutes, or until piping hot and cooked through. Turn the patties over halfway through the cooking time.

7 Serve the fish cakes immediately with the sweet chili sauce for dipping.

TASTY TIP

A horseradish dip could be used in place of sweet chili sauce. Mix together 2 tablespoons grated horseradish (from a jar) with 3 tablespoons each plain yogurt and mayonnaise. Add 3 finely chopped scallions, a squeeze of lime, and salt and pepper to taste.

1

2

5

Hoisin Chicken Pancakes

INGREDIENTS

Serves 4

3 tbsp. hoisin sauce

1 garlic clove, peeled and crushed

1-in. piece fresh ginger, peeled and
finely grated

1 tbsp. soy sauce

1 tsp. sesame oil

salt and freshly ground black pepper

4 skinless chicken thighs

½ cucumber, peeled (optional)

12 store-bought Chinese pancakes

6 scallions, trimmed and cut lengthwise

sweet chile dipping sauce, to serve

TASTY TIP

If you have a wheat allergy or want
to make this dish more substantial,
stir-fry the scallions and cucumber
pieces in a little peanut oil. Add a
carrot cut into matchsticks and mix
in the thinly sliced chicken and extra
marinade (as prepared in step 3).
Serve with steamed rice—Thai
fragrant rice is particularly good.

1 Preheat the oven to 375°F. In a nonmetallic bowl, mix the hoisin
sauce with the garlic, ginger, soy sauce, sesame oil, and seasoning.

2 Add the chicken thighs and coat in the mixture. Cover loosely with
plastic wrap and leave in the refrigerator to marinate for 3–4 hours,
turning the chicken occasionally.

3 Remove the chicken from the marinade and place in a roasting pan.
Set the marinade aside. Cook in the preheated oven for 30 minutes,
basting occasionally with the marinade.

4 Cut the cucumber in half lengthwise, and remove the seeds by
running a teaspoon down the center to scoop them out. Cut into
thin pieces.

5 Place the pancakes in a steamer to warm, according to the
instructions on the package. Thinly slice the hot chicken, and
arrange on a plate with the shredded scallions, cucumber, and
pancakes.

6 Place a spoonful of the chicken in the center of each warmed
pancake, and top with pieces of cucumber, scallion, and some of the
dipping sauce. Roll up and serve immediately.

2

4

5

Hot Herbed Mushrooms

INGREDIENTS

Serves 4

4 thin slices white bread, crusts
  removed
1¾ cups wiped and sliced crimini
  mushrooms
1¾ cups wiped oyster mushrooms
1 garlic clove, peeled and crushed
1 tsp. mustard
1¼ cups chicken stock
salt and freshly ground black pepper
1 tbsp. freshly chopped parsley
1 tbsp. freshly cut chives, plus extra
  to garnish
mixed lettuce leaves, to serve

FOOD FACT

Mushrooms are an extremely nutritious food because they are rich in the kind of vitamins and minerals that help to boost our immune system. This recipe could be adapted to include shiitake mushrooms. In studies, these were shown to strengthen the body's ability to protect itself from cancer.

1 Preheat the oven to 350°F. With a rolling pin, roll each piece of bread out as thinly as possible.

2 Press each piece of bread into a 4-inch tartlet pan. Push each piece firmly down, then bake in the preheated oven for 20 minutes.

3 Place the mushrooms in a skillet with the garlic, mustard, and chicken stock, and stir-fry over medium heat until the mushrooms are tender and the liquid is reduced by half.

4 Using a slotted spoon, carefully remove the mushrooms from the skillet, and transfer to a heat-resistant dish. Cover with foil and place in the bottom of the oven to keep the mushrooms warm.

5 Boil the remaining juices until reduced to a thick sauce. Season with salt and pepper.

6 Stir the parsley and chives into the mushroom mixture.

7 Place one bread tartlet shell on each plate, and divide the mushroom mixture among them.

8 Spoon over the juices, garnish with the chives, and serve immediately with mixed lettuce leaves.

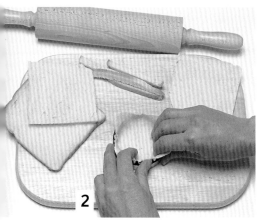

Cilantro Chicken & Soy Sauce Cakes

INGREDIENTS

Serves 4

¼ cucumber, peeled

1 shallot, peeled and thinly sliced

6 radishes, trimmed and sliced

12 oz. skinless, boneless chicken thighs

4 tbsp. coarsely chopped
   fresh cilantro

2 scallions, trimmed and
   coarsely chopped

1 red chile, seeded and chopped

2 tsp. finely grated lime zest

2 tbsp. soy sauce

1 tbsp. sugar

2 tbsp. rice vinegar

1 red chile, seeded and finely sliced

freshly chopped cilantro, to garnish

1   Preheat the oven to 375°F. Halve the peeled cucumber lengthwise, remove the seeds, and dice.

2   In a bowl, mix the shallot and radishes together. Keep chilled until ready to serve.

3   Place the chicken thighs in a food processor, and blend until coarsely chopped.

4   Add the cilantro and scallions to the chicken with the chile, lime zest, and soy sauce. Blend again until mixed.

5   Using slightly damp hands, shape the chicken mixture into 12 small rounds.

6   Place the rounds on a lightly greased baking sheet and cook in the preheated oven for 15 minutes, or until golden.

7   In a small saucepan, heat the sugar with 2 tablespoons water until dissolved. Simmer until syrupy.

8   Remove from the heat and let cool a little, then stir in the vinegar and chile slices. Pour over the cucumber, radish, and shallot salad. Garnish with the freshly chopped cilantro and serve the chicken cakes with the salad immediately.

FOOD FACT

The chicken cakes can be altered so that half chicken and half lean pork is used.

2

4

6

Roasted Eggplant Dip with Pitta Strips

INGREDIENTS

Serves 4

4 pita breads
2 large eggplants
1 garlic clove, peeled
¼ tsp. sesame oil
1 tbsp. lemon juice
½ tsp. ground cumin
salt and freshly ground black pepper
2 tbsp. freshly chopped parsley
mixed lettuce leaves, to serve

1 Preheat the oven to 350°F. On a cutting board, cut the pita breads into strips, and spread in a single layer onto a large baking sheet.

2 Cook in the preheated oven for 15 minutes, or until golden brown and crisp. Let cool on a wire rack.

3 Trim the eggplants, rinse lightly, and set aside. Heat a ridged grill pan until almost smoking. Cook the eggplants and garlic for about 15 minutes.

4 Turn the eggplants frequently until very tender, with wrinkled and charred skins. Remove from the heat and let cool.

5 When the eggplants are cool enough to handle, cut in half, and scoop out the cooked flesh, and place in a food processor.

6 Squeeze the softened garlic flesh from the papery skin, and add to the eggplant in the food processor.

7 Blend the eggplant and garlic until smooth, then add the sesame oil, lemon juice, and cumin, and blend again to mix.

8 Season to taste with salt and pepper, stir in the parsley, and serve with the pita strips and mixed lettuce leaves.

3

6

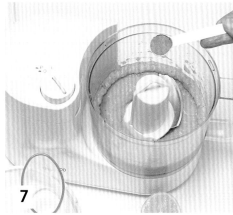
7

Grilled Garlic & Lemon Squid

INGREDIENTS

Serves 4

¹/₂ cup long-grain rice
1¹/₄ cups fish stock
8 oz. squid, cleaned
1 tbsp. grated lemon zest
1 garlic clove, peeled and crushed
1 shallot, peeled and finely chopped
2 tbsp. lemon juice
salt and freshly ground black pepper
2 tbsp. freshly chopped cilantro

HELPFUL HINT

To prepare squid, peel the tentacles from the squid's pouch, and cut away the head just below the eye. Discard the head. Remove the quill and the soft innards from the squid, and discard. Peel off any dark skin that covers the squid, and discard. Rinse the tentacles and pouch thoroughly. The squid is now ready to use.

1 Rinse the rice until the water runs clear, then place in a saucepan with the stock.

2 Bring to a boil, then reduce the heat. Cover and simmer gently for 10 minutes.

3 Turn off the heat and leave the saucepan covered so the rice can steam while you cook the squid.

4 Remove the tentacles from the squid, and set aside.

5 Cut the body cavity in half. Using the tip of a small, sharp knife, score the inside flesh of the body cavity in a diamond pattern. Do not cut all the way through.

6 Mix the lemon zest, crushed garlic, and chopped shallot together. Place the squid in a shallow bowl, sprinkle the lemon mixture on top, and stir.

7 Heat a ridged grill pan until almost smoking. Cook the squid for 3–4 minutes until cooked through, then slice.

8 Sprinkle with the lemon juice and season to taste with salt and pepper. Drain the rice and place the squid on top of it. Scatter the chopped cilantro over everything and serve.

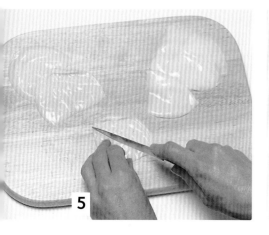

5

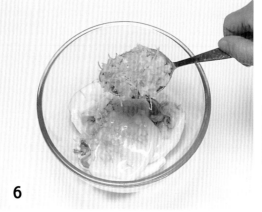

6

7

Creamy Salmon with Dill in Phyllo Baskets

INGREDIENTS

Serves 4

1 bay leaf
6 black peppercorns
1 large parsley sprig
6 oz. salmon fillet
4 large sheets phyllo pastry
fine spray of oil
2½ cups baby spinach leaves
8 tbsp. low-fat sour cream
2 tsp. mustard
2 tbsp. freshly chopped dill
salt and freshly ground black pepper

FOOD FACT

This is a highly nutritious dish, combining calcium-rich salmon with vitamin- and mineral-rich spinach. The low-fat sour cream in this recipe can be replaced with low-fat yogurt if you want to aid digestion and give your immune system a real boost!

1. Preheat the oven to 400°F. Place the bay leaf, peppercorns, parsley, and salmon in a large skillet, and add enough water to barely cover the fish.

2. Bring to a boil, reduce the heat, and cook the fish for 5 minutes until it flakes easily. Remove from the skillet and set aside.

3. Spray each sheet of phyllo pastry lightly with the oil. Scrunch up the pastry to make a nest shape approximately 5 inches in diameter.

4. Place on a lightly greased baking sheet, and cook in the preheated oven for 10 minutes until golden and crisp.

5. Blanch the baby spinach leaves in a saucepan of lightly salted boiling water for 2 minutes. Drain thoroughly and keep warm.

6. Mix the sour cream, mustard, and dill together, then warm gently. Season to taste with salt and pepper. Divide the spinach among the phyllo pastry nests, and flake the salmon onto the spinach.

7. Spoon the mustard and dill sauce over the phyllo pastry baskets and serve immediately.

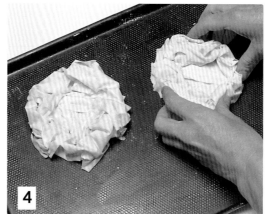
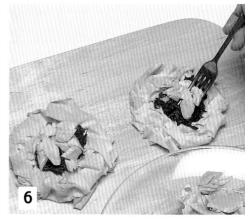

Smoked Salmon Sushi

INGREDIENTS

Serves 4

3/4 cup sushi rice

2 tbsp. rice vinegar

4 tsp. sugar

1/2 tsp salt

2 sheets sushi nori

2 1/2 oz. smoked salmon

1/4 cucumber, cut into fine strips

To serve:

wasabi

soy sauce

pickled ginger

TASTY TIP

If wasabi is unavailable, use a little horseradish. If you cannot find sushi nori (seaweed sheets), shape the rice into small bite-size oblongs, then drape a piece of smoked salmon over each one, and garnish with chives.

1. Rinse the rice thoroughly in cold water until the water runs clear, then place in a large saucepan with 1 1/4 cups water. Bring to a boil and cover with a tight-fitting lid. Reduce to a simmer and cook gently for 10 minutes. Turn the heat off, but keep the saucepan covered to allow the rice to steam for an additional 10 minutes.

2. In a small saucepan, gently heat the rice vinegar, sugar, and salt until the sugar has dissolved. When the rice has finished steaming, pour over the vinegar mixture and stir well to mix. Empty the rice out onto a large, flat surface (a cutting board or large plate is ideal). Fan the rice to cool and to produce a shinier rice.

3. Lay one sheet of sushi nori on a sushi mat (if you do not have a sushi mat, improvise with a stiff piece of fabric that is a little larger than the sushi nori), and spread with half the cooled rice. Dampen your hands while doing this, to prevent the rice from sticking to your hands. On the nearest edge, place half the salmon and half the cucumber strips.

4. Roll up the rice and smoked salmon tightly. Dampen the blade of a sharp knife and cut the sushi into slices about 3/4 inch thick. Repeat with the remaining sushi nori, rice, smoked salmon, and cucumber. Serve with wasabi, soy sauce, and pickled ginger.

2

3

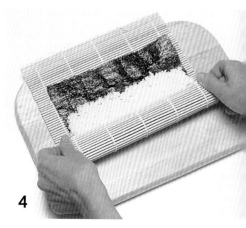

4

Asian Ground Chicken on Arugula & Tomato

INGREDIENTS

Serves 4

2 shallots, peeled
1 garlic clove, peeled
1 carrot, peeled
½ cup water chestnuts
1 tsp. oil
12 oz. fresh ground chicken
1 tsp. Chinese five spice powder
pinch of chile powder
1 tsp. soy sauce
1 tbsp. fish sauce
8 cherry tomatoes
1¼ cups arugula

TASTY TIP

To make this dish a main meal, replace the arugula and tomatoes with stir-fried vegetables and rice. Another alternative that works very well is to serve the chicken mixture in Step 3 in lettuce leaves. Place a spoonful of the mixture into a lettuce leaf and roll up into a small pocket.

1 Finely chop the shallots and garlic. Cut the carrot into matchsticks, thinly slice the water chestnuts, and set aside. Heat the oil in a large wok or heavy skillet, and add the chicken. Stir-fry for 3–4 minutes over medium-high heat, breaking up any large pieces of chicken.

2 Add the garlic and shallots and cook for 2–3 minutes until softened. Sprinkle with the Chinese five spice powder and chile powder, and continue to cook for about 1 minute.

3 Add the carrot, water chestnuts, soy and fish sauces, and 2 tablespoons water. Stir-fry for an additional 2 minutes. Remove from the heat and set aside to cool slightly.

4 Seed the tomatoes and cut into thin wedges. Toss with the arugula and divide among 4 serving plates. Spoon the warm chicken mixture over the arugula and tomato wedges, and serve immediately to keep the arugula from wilting.

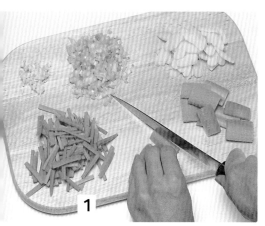

1

1

4

Sweet Potato Chips with Mango Salsa

INGREDIENTS

Serves 6

For the salsa:

1 large mango, peeled, pitted, and cut
    into small cubes
8 cherry tomatoes, quartered
½ cucumber, peeled and finely diced
1 red onion, peeled and
    finely chopped
pinch of sugar
1 red chile, seeded and
    finely chopped
2 tbsp. rice vinegar
2 tbsp. olive oil
grated zest and juice of 1 lime
2 tbsp. freshly chopped mint

For the potato chips:

$2^2/_3$ cups peeled and thinly sliced
    sweet potatoes
vegetable oil, for deep-frying
sea salt

1 To make the salsa, mix the mango with the tomatoes, cucumber, and onion. Add the sugar, chile, vinegar, olive oil, and the lime zest and juice. Mix together thoroughly, cover, and leave for 45–50 minutes.

2 Soak the sweet potatoes in cold water for 40 minutes to remove as much of the excess starch as possible. Drain and dry thoroughly on a clean dishtowel or paper towel.

3 Heat the vegetable oil to 375°F in a deep fryer. When at the correct temperature, place half the potatoes in the frying basket, then carefully lower the potatoes into the hot oil and cook for 4–5 minutes, or until they are golden brown. Shake the basket often so that the potatoes do not stick together.

4 Drain the potato chips on paper towels, sprinkle with sea salt, and place under a preheated broiler for a few seconds to dry out. Repeat with the remaining potatoes. Stir the mint into the salsa and serve with the potato chips.

1

3

4

Stuffed Grape Leaves

INGREDIENTS

Serves 6–8

heaping ³/₄ cup long-grain rice

½ lb. fresh or preserved grape leaves

1 red onion, peeled and
  finely chopped

3 baby leeks, trimmed and
  finely sliced

1 cup freshly chopped parsley

1 cup freshly chopped mint

1 cup freshly chopped dill

²/₃ cup extra-virgin olive oil

salt and freshly ground
  black pepper

¼ cup currants

½ cup finely chopped
  dried apricots

2½ tbsp. pine nuts

juice of 1 lemon

2½–3¼ cups boiling stock

lemon wedges or slices, to garnish

4 tbsp. plain yogurt, to serve

1 Soak the rice in cold water for 30 minutes. If using fresh grape leaves, blanch them, 5–6 leaves at a time, in salted, boiling water for a minute. Rinse and drain. If using preserved grape leaves, soak in tepid water for at least 20 minutes, drain, rinse, and pat dry with a paper towel.

2 Mix the onion and leeks with the herbs and half the olive oil. Add the drained rice, mix, and season with salt and pepper. Stir in the currants, apricots, pine nuts, and lemon juice. Spoon 1 teaspoon of the filling at the stalk end of each leaf. Roll, tucking the side flaps into the center to create a neat pocket. Continue until all the filling is used.

3 Layer half the remaining grape leaves over the bottom of a large skillet. Put the little pockets in the skillet, and cover with the remaining leaves.

4 Pour in enough stock just to cover the grape leaves, add a pinch of salt, and bring to a boil. Reduce the heat, cover, and simmer for 45–55 minutes, or until the rice is sticky and tender. Let stand for 10 minutes. Drain off any remaining stock. Garnish with lemon wedges or slices, and serve hot with the yogurt.

2

2

3

Potato Skins

INGREDIENTS

Serves 4

4 large baking potatoes
2 tbsp. olive oil
2 tsp. paprika, plus extra for sprinkling
¾ cup coarsely chopped pancetta
  or bacon
6 tbsp. heavy cream
⅓ cup diced blue cheese, such
  as Gorgonzola
1 tbsp. freshly chopped parsley

To serve:

mayonnaise
sweet chile dipping sauce
tossed green salad

FOOD FACT

A popular Italian cheese, Gorgonzola was first made more than 1,100 years ago in the village of the same name near Milan. Now mostly produced in Lombardy, it is made from pasteurized cows' milk and allowed to ripen for at least three months, giving it a rich but not overpowering flavor.

1 Preheat the oven to 400°F. Scrub the potatoes, then prick a few times with a fork or skewer and place directly on the top shelf of the oven. Bake in the preheated oven for at least 1 hour, or until tender. The potatoes are cooked when they yield gently to the pressure of your hand.

2 Set the potatoes aside until cool enough to handle, then cut in half and scoop the flesh into a bowl and set aside. Preheat the broiler, and line the pan with aluminum foil.

3 Mix together the olive oil and paprika, and use half to brush the outside of the potato skins. Place on the foil-lined pan under the preheated broiler, and cook for 5 minutes, or until crisp, turning as necessary.

4 Heat the remaining paprika-flavored oil and gently fry the pancetta until crisp. Add to the potato flesh along with the cream, blue cheese, and parsley. Halve the potato skins, and fill with the blue-cheese filling. Return to the oven for an additional 15 minutes to heat through. Sprinkle with a little more paprika, and serve immediately with mayonnaise, sweet chili sauce, and a green salad.

2

3

4

Rice & Papaya Salad

INGREDIENTS

Serves 4

1 cup easy-cook basmati rice

1 cinnamon stick, bruised

zest and juice of 2 limes

1 Thai chile, seeded and
  finely chopped

zest and juice of 2 lemons

2 tbsp. Thai fish sauce

1 tbsp. light brown sugar

1 papaya, peeled and seeded

1 mango, peeled and pitted

1 green chile, seeded and
  finely chopped

2 tbsp. freshly chopped cilantro

1 tbsp. freshly chopped mint

1¼ cups finely shredded cooked
  chicken meat

½ cup chopped roasted peanuts

pita bread strips, to serve

1 Rinse and drain the rice, and pour into a saucepan. Add 2 cups salted, boiling water and the cinnamon stick. Bring to a boil, reduce the heat to a very low setting, cover, and cook, without stirring, for 15–18 minutes, or until all the liquid is absorbed. The rice should be light and fluffy, and have steam holes on the surface. Remove the cinnamon stick and stir in the zest from 1 lime.

2 To make the dressing, place the Thai chile, remaining zest and lime and lemon juice, fish sauce, and sugar in a food processor, and mix for a few minutes until blended. Alternatively, place all these ingredients in an airtight jar and shake vigorously until well blended. Pour half the dressing over the hot rice and toss until the grains glisten.

3 Slice the papaya and mango into thin slices, then place in a bowl. Add the chopped green chile, cilantro, and mint. Add the cooked chicken to the bowl with the chopped peanuts.

4 Add the remaining dressing to the chicken mixture and stir until all the ingredients are lightly coated. Spoon the rice onto a platter, pile the chicken mixture on top, and serve with strips of warm pita bread.

HELPFUL HINT

The papaya's skin turns from green when unripe, through to yellow and orange.

1

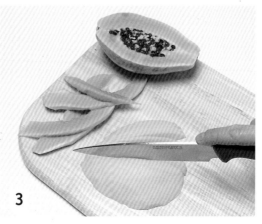

3

3

Chinese Pork in Pancake Wraps

INGREDIENTS

Serves 4

6 oz. pork tenderloin

2 tsp. Chinese rice wine or dry sherry

2 tbsp. light soy sauce

1 tsp. cornstarch

1 oz. dried tiger lily buds, soaked
  and drained

2 tbsp. peanut oil

3 large eggs, lightly beaten

1 tsp. freshly grated ginger

3 scallions, trimmed and thinly sliced

²/₃ cup bamboo shoots, in fine strips

salt and freshly ground black pepper

8 mandarin pancakes, steamed

hoisin sauce

cilantro sprigs, to garnish

HELPFUL HINT

Tiger lily buds, also known as "golden needles," are dried, unopened lily flowers. They are about 2 inches long, have a slightly furry texture, and are strongly fragrant. Buy those that are bright gold in color, and store in a cool, dark place.

1　Cut the pork across the grain into ½-inch slices, then cut into thin strips. Place in a bowl with the Chinese rice wine or sherry, soy sauce, and cornstarch. Mix well and set aside. Trim off the tough ends of the dried tiger lily buds, then cut in half and set aside.

2　Heat a wok or skillet, and add 1 tablespoon of the peanut oil. When hot, add the eggs, and cook for 1 minute, stirring constantly until scrambled. Remove and set aside. Wipe the wok clean with paper towels.

3　Return the wok to the heat, add the remaining oil, and, when hot, transfer the pork strips from the marinade mixture to the wok, shaking off as much marinade as possible. Stir-fry for 30 seconds, then add the ginger, scallions, and bamboo shoots, and pour in the marinade. Stir-fry for 2–3 minutes.

4　Return the scrambled eggs to the wok, season to taste with salt and pepper, and stir for a few seconds until mixed well and heated through. Divide the mixture between the pancakes, drizzle each with 1 teaspoon of hoisin sauce, and roll up. Garnish with sprigs of cilantro and serve immediately.

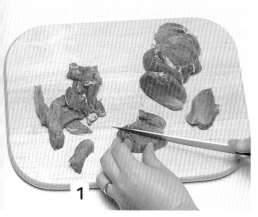

Crispy Pork Wontons

INGREDIENTS

Serves 4

1 small onion, peeled and
  coarsely chopped

2 garlic cloves, peeled and crushed

1 green chile, seeded and chopped

1-in. piece fresh ginger, peeled and
  coarsely chopped

1 lb. lean ground pork

4 tbsp. freshly chopped cilantro

1 tsp. Chinese five spice powder

salt and freshly ground black pepper

20 wonton wrappers

1 large egg, lightly beaten

vegetable oil, for deep-frying

sweet chili dipping sauce, to serve

HELPFUL HINT

When frying the wontons, use a deep, heavy saucepan or special deep fryer. Never fill the pan more than one-third full with oil. To check the temperature, either use a cooking thermometer, or drop a cube of day-old bread into the hot oil. It will turn golden brown in 45 seconds.

1 Place the onion, garlic, chile, and ginger in a food processor, and blend until very finely chopped. Add the pork, cilantro, and Chinese five spice powder. Season to taste with salt and pepper, then blend again briefly to mix. Divide the mixture into 20 equal portions and, with floured hands, shape each into a walnut-size ball.

2 Brush the edges of a wonton wrapper with beaten egg, place a pork ball in the center, then bring the corners to the center and pinch together to make a pouch. Repeat with the remaining pork balls and wrappers.

3 Pour enough vegetable oil into a heavy saucepan or deep fryer so that it is one-third full, and heat to 350°F. Deep-fry the wontons in three or four batches for 3–4 minutes, or until cooked through, golden, and crisp. Drain on paper towels. Serve the crispy pork wontons immediately, allowing five per person, with some sweet chili sauce for dipping.

1

2

3

Mixed Satay Sticks

INGREDIENTS

Serves 4

12 jumbo shrimp
³/₄ lb. beef steak
1 tbsp. lemon juice
1 garlic clove, peeled and crushed
salt
2 tsp. dark brown sugar
1 tsp. ground cumin
1 tsp. ground coriander
¹/₄ tsp. turmeric
1 tbsp. peanut oil
fresh cilantro leaves, to garnish

For the spicy peanut sauce:

1 shallot, peeled and very
  finely chopped
1 tsp. raw sugar
¹/₄ cup creamed coconut, chopped
pinch of chile powder
1 tbsp. dark soy sauce
¹/₂ cup crunchy peanut butter

1 Soak 8 bamboo skewers in cold water for at least 30 minutes. Peel the shrimp, leaving the tails on. Using a sharp knife, remove the black vein along the back of the shrimp. Cut the beef into strips ¹/₂ inch wide. Place the shrimp and beef in separate bowls, and sprinkle each with ¹/₂ tablespoon of the lemon juice.

2 Mix together the garlic, pinch of salt, sugar, cumin, coriander, turmeric and peanut oil to make a paste. Lightly brush over the shrimp and beef. Cover and place in the refrigerator to marinate for at least 30 minutes, but for longer if possible.

3 Meanwhile, make the sauce. Pour ¹/₂ cup water into a small saucepan, add the shallot and sugar, and heat gently until the sugar has dissolved. Stir in the creamed coconut and chile powder. When melted, remove from the heat and stir in the soy sauce and peanut butter. Let cool slightly, then spoon into a serving dish.

4 Preheat the broiler. Thread 3 shrimp onto each of 4 skewers, and divide the sliced beef between the remaining skewers.

5 Cook the skewers under the preheated broiler for 4–5 minutes, turning occasionally. The shrimp should be opaque and pink, and the beef browned on the outside, but still pink in the center. Transfer to warmed individual serving plates, garnish with a few fresh cilantro leaves, and serve immediately with the warm peanut sauce.

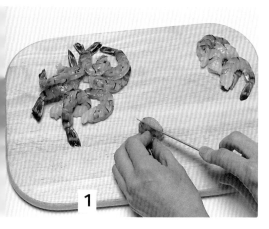

1

2

3

Corn Fritters

INGREDIENTS

Serves 4

4 tbsp. peanut oil
1 small onion, peeled and
  finely chopped
1 red chile, seeded and
  finely chopped
1 garlic clove, peeled and crushed
1 tsp. ground coriander
11 oz. canned corn
6 scallions, trimmed and
  finely sliced
1 large egg, lightly beaten
salt and freshly ground black pepper
3 tbsp. all-purpose flour
1 tsp. baking powder
scallion curls, to garnish
Thai-style chutney, to serve

1 Heat 1 tablespoon of the peanut oil in a skillet, add the onion, and cook gently for 7–8 minutes, or until beginning to soften. Add the chile, garlic, and ground coriander, and cook for 1 minute, stirring continuously. Remove from the heat.

2 Drain the corn and tip into a mixing bowl. Lightly crush with a potato masher to break down the corn a little. Add the cooked onion mixture to the bowl with the scallions and beaten egg. Season to taste with salt and pepper, then stir to mix together. Sift the flour and baking powder over the mixture and stir in.

3 Heat 2 tablespoons of the peanut oil in a large skillet. Drop 4 or 5 heaping teaspoonfuls of the corn mixture into the pan, and using a metal spatula or lifter, flatten each to make each fritter ½ inch thick.

4 Fry the fritters for 3 minutes, or until golden brown on the underside, turn over, and fry for an additional 3 minutes, or until cooked through and crisp.

5 Remove the fritters from the skillet and drain on paper towels. Keep warm while cooking the remaining fritters, adding a little more oil if needed. Garnish the fritters with scallion curls, and serve immediately with Thai-style chutney.

1

2

4

Sesame Shrimp Toasts

INGREDIENTS

Serves 4

³/₄ cup peeled, cooked shrimp

1 tbsp. cornstarch

2 scallions, peeled and
    coarsely chopped

2 tsp. freshly grated ginger

2 tsp. dark soy sauce

pinch of Chinese five spice
    powder (optional)

1 medium egg, beaten

salt and freshly ground black pepper

6 thin slices day-old white bread

3 tbsp. sesame seeds

vegetable oil, for deep-frying

sweet chili dipping sauce, to serve

HELPFUL HINT

The toasts can be prepared to the end of Step 3 up to 12 hours in advance. Cover with plastic wrap and chill in the refrigerator until needed. It is important to use bread that is a day or two old, not fresh bread. Make sure the shrimp are very well drained before pureeing them—pat them dry on paper towels, if necessary.

1 Place the shrimp in a food processor or blender with the cornstarch, scallions, ginger, soy sauce, and Chinese five spice powder. Blend to a fairly smooth paste. Spoon into a bowl and stir in the beaten egg. Season to taste with salt and pepper.

2 Cut the crusts off the bread. Spread the shrimp paste in an even layer on one side of each slice. Sprinkle over the sesame seeds, and press down lightly.

3 Cut each slice diagonally into 4 triangles. Place on a board and chill in the refrigerator for 30 minutes.

4 Pour enough vegetable oil into a heavy saucepan or deep fryer so that it is one-third full. Heat until it reaches a temperature of 350°F. Cook the toast in batches of 5 or 6, carefully lowering them seeded-side down into the oil. Deep-fry for 2–3 minutes, or until lightly browned, then turn over and cook for 1 more minute. Using a slotted spoon, lift out the pieces of toast, and drain on paper towels. Keep warm while frying the remaining pieces. Arrange on a warmed platter, and serve immediately with some chili sauce for dipping.

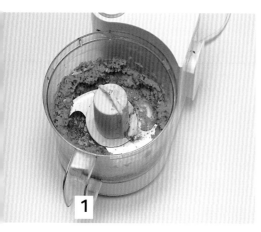
1

2

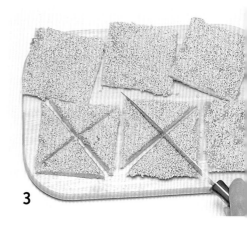
3

Sweet & Sour Battered Fish

INGREDIENTS

Serves 4–6

1 lb. white fish fillet, skinned
1½ cups all-purpose flour
salt and freshly ground black pepper
2 tbsp. cornstarch
2 tbsp. arrowroot
vegetable oil, for deep-frying

For the sweet & sour sauce:

4 tbsp. orange juice
2 tbsp. white wine vinegar
2 tbsp. dry sherry
1 tbsp. dark soy sauce
1 tbsp. golden brown sugar
2 tsp. tomato paste
1 red bell pepper, seeded and diced
2 tsp. cornstarch

TASTY TIP

Any firm white fish can be used for this dish, as long as it is fairly thick. Your fish retailer can tell you which varieties are suitable.

1 Cut the fish into 1 x 2-inch pieces. Place 4 tablespoons of the flour in a small bowl, season with salt and pepper to taste, then add the fish strips, a few at a time, tossing until coated.

2 Sift the remaining flour into a bowl with a pinch of salt, the cornstarch, and arrowroot. Gradually whisk in 2½ cups ice water to make a smooth, thin batter.

3 Heat the vegetable oil in a wok or deep fryer to 375°F. Working in batches, dip the fish strips in the batter, and deep-fry them for 3–5 minutes, or until crisp. Using a slotted spoon, remove the strips, and drain on paper towels.

4 Meanwhile, make the sauce. Place 3 tablespoons of the orange juice, the vinegar, sherry, soy sauce, sugar, tomato paste, and red bell pepper in a small saucepan. Bring to a boil, reduce the heat, and simmer for 3 minutes.

5 Blend the cornstarch with the remaining orange juice, stir into the sauce, and simmer, stirring, for 1 minute or until thickened. Arrange the fish on a warmed platter or individual plates. Drizzle with a little of the sauce, and serve immediately with the remaining sauce.

1

2

5

Spicy Beef Pancakes

INGREDIENTS

Serves 4

½ cup all-purpose flour
pinch of salt
½ tsp. Chinese five spice powder
1 extra-large egg yolk
⅔ cup milk
4 tsp. sunflower oil
scallion slices, to garnish

For the spicy beef filling:

1 tbsp. sesame oil
4 scallions, sliced
½-in. piece fresh ginger, peeled and
  finely grated
1 garlic clove, peeled and crushed
¾ lb. sirloin steak, trimmed and cut
  into strips
1 red chile, seeded and
  finely chopped
1 tsp. sherry vinegar
1 tsp. dark brown sugar
1 tbsp. dark soy sauce

1 Sift the flour, salt, and Chinese five spice powder into a bowl, and make a well in the center. Add the egg yolk and a little of the milk. Gradually beat in, drawing in the flour to make a smooth batter. Whisk in the rest of the milk.

2 Heat 1 teaspoon of the sunflower oil in a small, heavy skillet. Pour in just enough batter to thinly coat the bottom of the pan. Cook over medium heat for 1 minute, or until the underside of the pancake is golden brown.

3 Turn or toss the pancake, and cook for 1 minute, or until the other side of the pancake is golden brown. Make 7 more pancakes with the remaining batter. Stack them on a warmed plate as you make them, with wax paper between each pancake. Cover with aluminum foil and keep warm in a low oven.

4 Make the filling. Heat a wok or large skillet, add the sesame oil, and when hot, add the scallions, ginger, and garlic, and stir-fry for 1 minute. Add the beef strips, stir-fry for 3–4 minutes, then stir in the chile, vinegar, sugar, and soy sauce. Cook for 1 minute, then remove from the heat.

5 Spoon one-eighth of the filling over one half of each pancake. Fold the pancakes in half, then fold in half again. Garnish the pancakes with a few slices of scallion and serve immediately.

2

4

5

Lion's Head Pork Balls

INGREDIENTS

Serves 4

½ cup glutinous rice
1 lb. lean ground pork
2 garlic cloves, peeled
  and crushed
1 tbsp. cornstarch
½ tsp. Chinese five spice powder
2 tsp. dark soy sauce
1 tbsp. Chinese rice wine or
  dry sherry
2 tbsp. freshly chopped cilantro
salt and freshly ground black pepper

For the sweet chili dipping sauce:

2 tsp. superfine sugar
1 tbsp. sherry vinegar
1 tbsp. light soy sauce
1 shallot, peeled and very
  finely chopped
1 small red chile, seeded and
  finely chopped
2 tsp. sesame oil

FOOD FACT

These meatballs get their name from the rice coating, which is thought to resemble a lion's mane.

1 Place the rice in a bowl, and pour in plenty of cold water. Cover and soak for 2 hours. Tip into a strainer and drain well.

2 Place the pork, garlic, cornstarch, Chinese five spice powder, soy sauce, Chinese rice wine or sherry, and cilantro in a bowl. Season to taste with salt and pepper, and mix together.

3 With slightly damp hands, shape the pork mixture into 20 walnut-size balls, then roll in the rice to coat. Place the balls slightly apart in a steamer or a colander set over a saucepan of boiling water, cover, and steam for 20 minutes, or until cooked through.

4 Meanwhile, make the dipping sauce. Stir together the sugar, vinegar, and soy sauce until the sugar dissolves. Add the shallot, chile, and sesame oil, and whisk together with a fork. Transfer to a small serving bowl, cover, and let stand for at least 10 minutes before serving.

5 Remove the pork balls from the steamer, and arrange them on a warmed serving platter. Serve immediately with the sweet chili dipping sauce.

1

3

4

Hot & Sour Squid

INGREDIENTS

Serves 4

8 baby squid, cleaned
2 tbsp. dark soy sauce
2 tbsp. hoisin sauce
1 tbsp. lime juice
2 tbsp. dry sherry
1 tbsp. honey
1-in. piece fresh ginger, peeled and
    finely chopped
1 red chile, seeded and
    finely chopped
1 green chile, seeded and
    finely chopped
1 tsp. cornstarch
salt and freshly ground black pepper
vegetable oil, for deep-frying
lime wedges, to garnish

HELPFUL HINT

It is simple to prepare squid. Rinse well in cold water, then firmly pull apart the head and body; the innards will come away with the head. Remove and discard the transparent beak. Rinse the body pouch thoroughly under cold running water and peel off the thin layer of dark skin.

1 Slice open the body of each squid lengthwise, open out, and place on a cutting board with the inside facing up. Using a knife, cut lightly in a crisscross pattern. Cut each one into 4 pieces. Trim the tentacles.

2 Place the soy and hoisin sauces with the lime juice, sherry, honey, ginger, chiles, and cornstarch in a bowl. Season to taste with salt and pepper, and mix together. Add the squid, stir well to coat, then cover and place in the refrigerator to marinate for 1 hour.

3 Tip the squid into a strainer over a small saucepan and strain off the marinade. Scrape any bits of chile or ginger into the saucepan, as they will burn if fried.

4 Fill a deep fryer one-third full with vegetable oil, and heat to 350°F. Deep-fry the squid in batches for 2–3 minutes, or until golden and crisp. Remove the squid and drain on paper towels. Keep warm.

5 Bring the marinade to a boil, and let it boil gently for a few seconds. Arrange the squid on a serving dish, and drizzle with the marinade. Garnish with lime wedges and serve immediately.

1

2

4

Spicy Shrimp in Lettuce Cups

INGREDIENTS

Serves 4

1 lemongrass stalk

1½ cups peeled cooked shrimp

1 tsp. finely grated lime zest

1 red Thai chile, seeded and finely
  chopped

1-in. piece fresh ginger, peeled and
  finely grated

2 heads romaine lettuce, divided
  into leaves

¼ cup chopped roasted peanuts

2 scallions, trimmed and
  diagonally sliced

cilantro sprigs, to garnish

For the coconut sauce:

2 tbsp. freshly grated coconut or
  unsweetened shredded dry coconut

1 tbsp. hoisin sauce

1 tbsp. light soy sauce

1 tbsp. Thai fish sauce

1 tbsp. soft golden brown sugar

1. Remove 3 or 4 of the tougher outer leaves of the lemongrass, and set aside for another dish. Finely chop the remaining soft center. Place 2 teaspoons of the chopped lemongrass in a bowl with the shrimp, grated lime zest, chile, and ginger. Mix together to coat the shrimp. Cover, and place in the refrigerator to marinate while you make the coconut sauce.

2. For the sauce, place the coconut in a wok and fry for 2–3 minutes, or until golden. Remove from the pan and set aside. Add the hoisin, soy, and fish sauces to the wok with the sugar and 4 tablespoons water. Simmer for 2–3 minutes, then remove from the heat. Let cool.

3. Pour the sauce over the shrimp, add the toasted coconut, and toss to mix together. Divide the shrimp and coconut sauce mixture between the romaine leaves and arrange on a platter.

4. Sprinkle with the peanuts and scallions and garnish with a sprig of cilantro. Serve immediately.

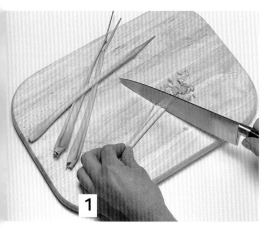

Cantonese Chicken Wings

INGREDIENTS

Serves 4

3 tbsp. hoisin sauce

2 tbsp. dark soy sauce

1 tbsp. sesame oil

1 garlic clove, peeled and crushed

1-in. piece fresh ginger, peeled and finely grated

1 tbsp. Chinese rice wine or dry sherry

2 tsp. chile bean sauce

2 tsp. red or white wine vinegar

2 tbsp. golden brown sugar

2 lb. large chicken wings

1/2 cup chopped cashews

2 scallions, trimmed and finely chopped

HELPFUL HINT

Chicken wings are regarded as a delicacy in both China and Thailand. If you give your butcher advance notice, he will probably sell them to you very cheaply, as they are often trimmed off and discarded when cutting chickens into portions.

1 Preheat the oven to 425°F. Place the hoisin sauce, soy sauce, sesame oil, garlic, ginger, Chinese rice wine or sherry, chile bean sauce, vinegar, and sugar in a small saucepan with 6 tablespoons water. Bring to a boil, stirring occasionally, then reduce the heat and simmer for about 30 seconds. Remove the glaze from the heat.

2 Place the chicken wings in a roasting pan in a single layer. Pour the glaze on top, and stir until the wings are coated thoroughly.

3 Cover the pan loosely with aluminum foil, place in the preheated oven, and roast for 25 minutes. Remove the foil, baste the wings, and cook for an additional 5 minutes.

4 Reduce the oven temperature to 375°F. Turn the wings over, and sprinkle with the chopped cashews and scallions. Return to the oven and cook for 5 minutes, or until the nuts are lightly browned, the glaze is sticky, and the wings are tender. Remove from the oven and let stand for 5 minutes before arranging on a warmed platter. Serve immediately with plenty of napkins.

1

2

4

Vegetable Thai Spring Rolls

INGREDIENTS

Serves 4

2 oz. cellophane vermicelli

4 dried shiitake mushrooms

1 tbsp. peanut oil

2 medium carrots, peeled and
thinly sliced

2 cups whole snow peas, cut
lengthwise into fine strips

3 scallions, trimmed and chopped

1/2 cup thinly sliced canned
bamboo shoots

1/2-in. piece fresh ginger, peeled and
finely grated

1 tbsp. light soy sauce

1 large egg, separated

salt and freshly ground black pepper

20 spring roll wrappers, each about
5 in. square

vegetable oil, for deep-frying

scallion tassels, to garnish

1 Place the vermicelli in a bowl and add enough boiling water to cover. Let soak for 5 minutes, or until softened, then drain. Cut into pieces 3 inches long. Soak the shiitake mushrooms in almost-boiling water for 15 minutes, drain, discard the stalks, and slice thinly.

2 Heat a wok or large skillet, add the peanut oil, and, when hot, add the carrots, and stir-fry for 1 minute. Add the snow peas and scallions, and stir-fry for 2–3 minutes, or until the vegetables are tender. Tip the vegetables into a bowl and let cool.

3 Stir the vermicelli and shiitake mushrooms into the cooled vegetables with the bamboo shoots, ginger, soy sauce, and egg yolk. Season to taste with salt and pepper, and mix thoroughly.

4 Brush the edges of a spring roll wrapper with a little beaten egg white. Spoon 2 teaspoons of the vegetable filling onto the wrapper, in a 3-inch log shape, 1 inch from one edge. Fold the wrapper edge over the filling, then fold in the right and left sides. Brush the folded edges with more egg white, and roll up neatly. Place on a greased cookie sheet, seam-side down, and make the rest of the spring rolls.

5 Heat the vegetable oil in a heavy saucepan or deep fryer to 350°F. Deep-fry the spring rolls, 6 at a time, for 2–3 minutes, or until golden brown and crisp. Drain on paper towels and arrange on a warmed platter. Garnish with scallion tassels and serve immediately.

1

2

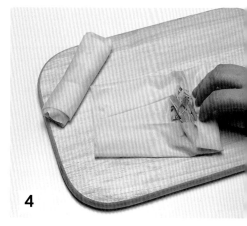

4

Crispy Shrimp with Chinese Dipping Sauce

INGREDIENTS

Serves 4

1 lb. medium-size shrimp, peeled

¼ tsp. salt

6 tbsp. peanut oil

2 garlic cloves, peeled and
  finely chopped

1-in. piece fresh ginger, peeled and
  finely chopped

1 green chile, seeded and
  finely chopped

4 stems cilantro, leaves and stems
  roughly chopped

For Chinese dipping sauce:

3 tbsp. dark soy sauce

3 tbsp. rice wine vinegar

1 tbsp. superfine sugar

2 tbsp. chili oil

2 scallions, finely shredded

1   Using a sharp knife, remove the black veins along the back of the shrimp. Sprinkle the shrimp with the salt, and let stand for 15 minutes. Pat dry on paper towels.

2   Heat a wok or large skillet, add the peanut oil, and, when hot, add the shrimp and stir-fry in 2 batches for about 1 minute, or until they turn pink, and are almost cooked. Using a slotted spoon, remove the shrimp, and set aside in a warm oven.

3   Drain the oil from the wok, leaving 1 tablespoon. Add the garlic, ginger, and chile, and cook for about 30 seconds. Add the cilantro, return the shrimp, and stir-fry for 1–2 minutes, or until the shrimp are cooked through and the garlic is golden. Turn into a warmed serving dish.

4   For the dipping sauce, beat together the soy sauce, rice vinegar, sugar, and chile oil in a small bowl with a fork. Stir in the scallions. Serve immediately with the hot shrimp.

2

3

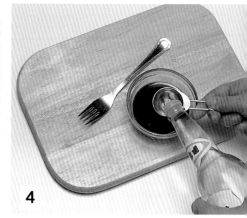

4

Poached Fish Dumplings with Creamy Chili Sauce

INGREDIENTS

Serves 4

1 lb. white fish fillet, skinned
   and boned
1 tsp. dark soy sauce
1 tbsp. cornstarch
1 large egg yolk
salt and freshly ground black pepper
3 tbsp. freshly chopped cilantro
6½ cups fish stock

For the creamy chili sauce:

2 tsp. peanut oil
2 garlic cloves, peeled and
   finely chopped
4 scallions, trimmed and finely sliced
2 tbsp. dry sherry
1 tbsp. sweet chili sauce
1 tbsp. light soy sauce
1 tbsp. lemon juice
6 tbsp. crème fraîche or sour cream

To garnish:

cilantro sprigs
fresh carrot sticks

1 Chop the fish into chunks, and place in a food processor with the soy sauce, cornstarch, and egg yolk. Season to taste with salt and pepper. Blend until fairly smooth. Add the cilantro and process for a few seconds until well mixed. Transfer to a bowl, cover, and chill in the refrigerator for 30 minutes.

2 With damp hands, shape the chilled mixture into walnut-size balls, and place on a cookie sheet lined with nonstick baking parchment. Chill in the refrigerator for an additional 30 minutes.

3 Pour the stock into a wide saucepan, bring to a boil, then reduce the heat until barely simmering. Add the fish dumplings and poach for 3–4 minutes, or until cooked through.

4 Meanwhile, to make the sauce, heat the peanut oil in a small saucepan, add the garlic and scallions, and cook until golden. Stir in the sherry, chile and soy sauces, and lemon juice, then remove immediately from the heat. Stir in the crème fraîche, and season to taste with salt and pepper.

5 Using a slotted spoon, lift the cooked fish dumplings from the stock and place on a warmed serving dish. Drizzle with the sauce, garnish with sprigs of cilantro and carrot sticks, and serve immediately.

1

2

3

Sesame Shrimp

INGREDIENTS

Serves 6–8

24 large shrimp
¼ cup all-purpose flour
4 tbsp. sesame seeds
salt and freshly ground black pepper
1 extra-large egg
1 cup vegetable oil, for deep-frying

For the soy dipping sauce:

¼ cup soy sauce
1 scallion, trimmed and
  finely chopped
½ tsp. dried crushed chiles
1 tbsp. sesame oil
1–2 tsp. sugar, or to taste

scallion strips, to garnish

HELPFUL HINT

Uncooked shrimp are widely available, but are least expensive when purchased frozen in boxes from seafood retailers.

1   Remove the heads from the shrimp by twisting away from the body, and discard. Peel the shrimp, leaving the tails on for presentation. Using a sharp knife, remove the black vein from the back of the shrimp. Rinse and dry.

2   Slice along the back, but do not cut through the body. Place on the cutting board, and press firmly to flatten slightly to make a butterfly shape.

3   Put the flour, half the sesame seeds, salt, and pepper into a food processor, and blend for 30 seconds. Tip into a plastic bag or a plastic container and add the shrimp, 4 or 5 at a time. Mix to coat with the flour.

4   Beat the egg in a small bowl with the remaining sesame seeds, salt, and pepper.

5   Heat the vegetable oil in a large wok to 375°F or until a small cube of bread browns in about 30 seconds. Working in batches of 5 or 6, and holding each shrimp by the tail, dip into the beaten egg, then carefully lower into the oil.

6   Cook for 1–2 minutes, or until crisp and golden, turning once or twice. Using a slotted spoon, remove the shrimp, drain on absorbent paper towels, and keep warm.

7   To make the dipping sauce, stir together the soy sauce, scallion, chiles, oil, and sugar until the sugar dissolves. Arrange the shrimp on a plate, garnish with strips of scallion, and serve immediately.

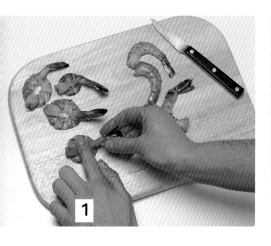

1

3

6

Steamed Barbecue Pork Balls

INGREDIENTS

Serves 12

For the buns:

1½–1¾ cups all-purpose flour
1 tbsp. rapid-rise active dry yeast
½ cup milk
2 tbsp. corn oil
1 tbsp. sugar
½ tsp. salt
scallion tassels, to garnish
salad greens, to serve

For the filling:

2 tbsp. vegetable oil
1 small red bell pepper, seeded and
  finely chopped
2 garlic cloves, peeled and
  finely chopped
2½ cups finely chopped cooked pork
¼ cup firmly packed light
  brown sugar
¼ cup ketchup
1–2 tsp. hot chili powder

1 Put ¾ cup of the flour in a bowl and stir in the yeast. Heat the milk, corn oil, sugar, and salt in a small saucepan until warm, stirring until the sugar has dissolved. Pour into the bowl, and with an electric mixer, beat on low speed for 30 seconds, scraping down the sides of the bowl until blended. Beat at high speed for 3 minutes, then with a wooden spoon, stir in as much of the remaining flour as possible until a stiff dough forms. Shape into a ball, place in a greased bowl, cover with plastic wrap, and leave for 1 hour in a warm place, or until doubled in size.

2 To make filling, heat a wok, add the vegetable oil, and, when hot, add the red bell pepper and garlic. Stir-fry for 4–5 minutes. Add the remaining ingredients and bring to a boil, stir-frying for 2–3 minutes until thick and syrupy. Cool and set aside.

3 Punch down the dough and turn onto a lightly floured surface. Divide into 12 pieces and shape them into balls, then cover and let rest for 5 minutes.

4 Roll each ball into a 3-inch circle. Place a heaping tablespoon of filling in the center of each. Dampen the edges, then bring them up and around the filling, pinching together to seal. Place seam-side down on a small square of nonstick baking parchment. Continue with the remaining dough and filling. Let rise for 10 minutes.

5 Bring a large wok half-filled with water to a boil, and place the buns on a lightly greased steamer, without touching each other. Cover and steam for 20–25 minutes, then remove and let cool. Garnish with scallion tassels and serve with salad greens.

1

4

5

Chicken-Filled Spring Rolls

INGREDIENTS

Makes 12–14 rolls

For the filling:
1 tbsp. vegetable oil

2 slices bacon, diced

½ lb. skinless chicken breast fillets, thinly sliced

1 small red bell pepper, seeded and finely chopped

4 scallions, trimmed and finely chopped

1-in. piece fresh ginger, peeled and finely chopped

¾ cup thinly sliced snow peas

¾ cup bean sprouts

1 tbsp. soy sauce

2 tsp. Chinese rice wine or dry sherry

2 tsp. hoisin or plum sauce

For the wrappers:
3 tbsp. all-purpose flour

12–14 spring roll wrappers

1 cup vegetable oil, for deep-frying

shredded scallions, to garnish

dipping sauce, to serve

1 Heat a large wok, add the vegetable oil, and, when hot, add the bacon and stir-fry for 2–3 minutes, or until golden. Add the chicken and bell pepper, and stir-fry for an additional 2–3 minutes. Add the remaining filling ingredients and stir-fry for 3–4 minutes until the vegetables are tender. Turn into a strainer and let drain as the mixture cools.

2 Blend the flour with about 1½ tablespoons water to form a paste. Soften each wrapper in a plate of warm water for 1–2 seconds, then place on a cutting board. Put 2–3 tablespoons of filling on the near edge. Fold the edge over the filling to cover. Fold in each side and roll up. Seal the edge with a little flour paste and press to seal. Transfer to a baking sheet, seam-side down.

3 Heat the vegetable oil in a large wok to 375°F or until a small cube of bread browns in about 30 seconds. Working in batches of 3 or 4, deep-fry the spring rolls until they are crisp and golden, turning once (about 2 minutes). Remove and drain on absorbent paper towels. Arrange the spring rolls on a serving plate, garnish with scallion tassels, and serve hot with dipping sauce.

Shrimp Salad with Toasted Rice

INGREDIENTS

Serves 4

For the dressing:
¼ cup rice vinegar
1 red chile, seeded and thinly sliced
3-in. piece lemongrass stalk, bruised
1 tbsp. lime juice
2 tbsp. Thai fish sauce
1 tsp. sugar, or to taste

For the salad:
¾ lb. large shrimp, peeled, with tails
  attached and heads removed
salt and freshly ground black pepper
cayenne pepper
1 tbsp. long-grain white rice
2 tbsp. corn oil
1 large head Chinese cabbage or
  romaine lettuce, shredded
½ small cucumber, peeled, seeded,
  and thinly sliced
1 small bunch chives, cut into
  1-in. pieces
small bunch mint leaves

1 Place all the ingredients for the dressing in a small bowl and let stand to allow the flavors to blend together.

2 Using a sharp knife, split each shrimp lengthwise in half, leaving the tail attached to one half. Remove any black veins and pat the shrimp dry with absorbent paper towels. Sprinkle the shrimp with a little salt and cayenne pepper, and then set aside.

3 Heat a wok over a high heat. Add the rice and stir-fry until browned and fragrant. Turn into a mortar and cool. Crush gently with a pestle until coarse crumbs form. Wipe the wok clean.

4 Reheat the wok, add the corn oil, and, when hot, add the shrimp and stir-fry for 2 minutes, or until pink. Transfer to a plate and season to taste with salt and pepper.

5 Place the Chinese cabbage or lettuce into a salad bowl with the cucumber, chives, and mint leaves, and toss lightly together.

6 Remove the lemongrass stalk and some of the chile from the dressing, and pour all but 2 tablespoons over the salad and toss until lightly coated. Add the shrimp and drizzle with the remaining dressing, then sprinkle with the toasted rice, and serve.

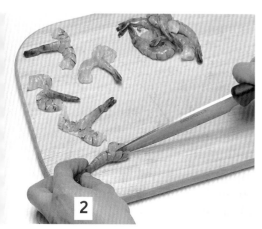

2

3

4

Sticky Braised Spareribs

INGREDIENTS

Serves 4

2 lb. spareribs, cut crosswise into
  3-in. pieces
½ cup orange juice
¼ cup dry white wine
3 tbsp. black bean sauce
3 tbsp. ketchup
2 tbsp. honey
3–4 scallions, trimmed and chopped
2 garlic cloves, peeled and crushed
1 tbsp. grated orange zest
salt and freshly ground black pepper

To garnish:

scallion tassels
lemon wedges

HELPFUL HINT

Boiling the ribs before cooking them in the sauce reduces the fat content and ensures that they are tender and more succulent.

1 Put the spareribs in the wok and add enough cold water to cover. Bring to a boil over medium-high heat, skimming any scum that rises to the surface. Cover and simmer for 30 minutes, then drain and rinse the ribs.

2 Rinse and dry the wok and return the ribs to it. In a bowl, blend the orange juice with the white wine, black bean sauce, tomato ketchup, and the honey until smooth.

3 Stir in the scallions, garlic, and grated orange zest. Stir well until mixed thoroughly.

4 Pour the mixture over the spareribs in the wok and stir gently until the ribs are lightly coated. Place over medium heat and bring to a boil.

5 Cover then simmer, stirring occasionally, for 1 hour, or until the ribs are tender and the sauce is thickened and sticky. If the sauce reduces too quickly or begins to stick, add water 1 tablespoon at a time until the ribs are tender. Adjust the seasoning to taste, then transfer the ribs to a serving plate and garnish with scallion tassels and lemon wedges. Serve immediately.

1

2

4

Shredded Duck in Lettuce Leaves

INGREDIENTS

Serves 4–6

2 tbsp. dried shiitake mushrooms

2 tbsp. vegetable oil

1 lb. boneless, skinless duck breast, cut
  crosswise into thin strips

1 red chile, seeded and thinly sliced
  diagonally

4–6 scallions, trimmed and
  sliced diagonally

2 garlic cloves, peeled and crushed

$^3/_4$ cup bean sprouts

3 tbsp. soy sauce

1 tbsp. Chinese rice wine or dry sherry

1–2 tsp. honey or brown sugar

4–6 tbsp. hoisin or plum sauce

large, crisp lettuce leaves, such
  as romaine

handful mint leaves

dipping sauce (see Sesame Shrimp,
  page 132)

FOOD FACT

Hoisin sauce is a sweet and spicy
Chinese sauce that is made
primarily from soybeans, sugar,
garlic, and chile.

1 Cover the dried shiitake mushrooms with almost boiling water, leave
   for 20 minutes, then drain and slice thinly.

2 Heat a large wok, add the vegetable oil and, when hot, stir-fry the
   duck for 3–4 minutes, or until sealed. Remove with a slotted spoon
   and set aside.

3 Add the chile, scallions, garlic and shiitake mushrooms to the wok
   and stir-fry for 2–3 minutes, or until softened.

4 Add the bean sprouts, soy sauce, Chinese rice wine or sherry
   and honey or brown sugar to the wok, and continue to stir-fry for
   1 minute, or until blended.

5 Stir in the reserved duck and stir-fry for 2 minutes, or until well
   mixed together and heated right through. Transfer to a heated
   serving dish.

6 Arrange the hoisin or plum sauce in a small bowl on a tray or plate
   with a pile of lettuce leaves and the mint leaves.

7 Let each guest spoon a little hoisin or plum sauce onto a lettuce
   leaf, then top with a large spoonful of the stir-fried duck and
   vegetables and roll up the leaf to enclose the filling. Serve with
   the dipping sauce.

Swedish Cocktail Meatballs

INGREDIENTS

Serves 4–6

4 tbsp. butter

1 onion, peeled and finely chopped

½ cup fresh white bread crumbs

1 large egg, beaten

½ cup heavy cream

salt and freshly ground black pepper

1½ cups fresh lean ground beef

½ cup fresh ground pork

3–4 tbsp. freshly chopped dill

½ tsp. ground allspice

1 tbsp. vegetable oil

½ cup beef stock

cream cheese and chive or cranberry
   sauce, to serve

1 Heat half the butter in a large wok, add the onion, and cook, stirring frequently, for 4–6 minutes, or until softened and beginning to color. Transfer to a bowl and let cool. Wipe out the wok with absorbent paper towels. Add the bread crumbs and beaten egg with 1–2 tablespoons of cream to the softened onion. Season to taste with salt and pepper and stir until well blended. Using your fingertips, crumble the ground beef and pork into the bowl.

2 Add half the dill, the allspice, and, using your hands, mix together until well blended. With damp hands, shape the mixture into 1-inch balls.

3 Melt the remaining butter in the wok and add the vegetable oil, swirling it to coat the sides of the wok. Working in batches, add about one-quarter to one-third of the meatballs in a single layer and cook for 5 minutes, swirling and turning until golden and cooked.

4 Transfer to a plate and continue with the remaining meatballs, transferring them to the plate as they are cooked. Pour off the fat in the wok. Add the beef stock and bring to a boil, then boil until reduced by half, stirring and scraping up any browned bits from the bottom. Add the remaining cream and continue to simmer until slightly thickened and reduced.

5 Stir in the remaining dill and season if necessary. Add the meatballs and simmer for 2–3 minutes, or until heated all the way through. Serve on toothpicks, with the sauce in a separate bowl for dipping.

1

2

3

Dim Sum Pork Bundles

INGREDIENTS

Makes about 40

$\frac{1}{2}$ cup drained and finely chopped
canned water chestnuts

$\frac{3}{4}$ cup shrimp, peeled, deveined, and
coarsely chopped

12 oz. ground pork

2 tbsp. smoked bacon, finely chopped

1 tbsp. light soy sauce, plus extra
to serve

1 tsp. dark soy sauce

1 tbsp. Chinese rice wine

2 tbsp. finely chopped fresh
peeled ginger

3 scallions, trimmed and
finely chopped

2 tsp. sesame oil

1 large egg white, lightly beaten

salt and freshly ground black pepper

2 tsp. sugar

40 wonton squares, thawed if frozen

toasted sesame seeds, to garnish

soy sauce, to serve

1 Place the water chestnuts, shrimp, pork, and bacon in a bowl, and mix together. Add the soy sauces, Chinese rice wine, ginger, chopped scallions, sesame oil, and egg white. Season to taste with salt and pepper, sprinkle in the sugar, and mix the filling thoroughly.

2 Place a spoonful of filling in the center of a wonton square. Bring the sides up, and press around the filling to make a basket shape. Flatten the base of the skin so that the wonton stands solid. The top should be wide open, exposing the filling.

3 Place the pockets on a heatproof plate, on a wire rack for a wok, or on the bottom of a cheesecloth-lined bamboo steamer. Place over a wok, half-filled with boiling water, cover, then steam the pockets for about 20 minutes. Do this in 2 batches. Transfer to a warmed serving plate, sprinkle with toasted sesame seeds, drizzle with soy sauce, and serve immediately.

1

2

3

Mixed Canapés

INGREDIENTS

Serves 12

For the stir-fried cheese:

6 thick slices white bread

3 tbsp. butter, softened

$^3/_4$ cup shredded sharp cheddar cheese

$^3/_4$ cup blue cheese, such as Gorgonzola, crumbled

3 tbsp. corn oil

For the spicy nuts:

2 tbsp. unsalted butter

2 tbsp. light olive oil

4 cups mixed unsalted nuts

1 tsp. ground paprika

$^1/_2$ tsp. ground cumin

$^1/_2$ tsp. fine sea salt

cilantro sprigs, to garnish

1 For the cheese canapés, cut the crusts off the bread, then gently roll with a rolling pin to flatten slightly. Spread thinly with butter, then sprinkle with the mixed cheeses as evenly as possible.

2 Roll up each slice tightly, then cut into 4 slices, each about 1 inch long. Heat the corn oil in a wok or large skillet and stir-fry the cheese rolls in two batches, turning them all the time until golden brown and crisp. Drain on absorbent paper towels and serve warm or cold.

3 For the spicy nuts, melt the butter and olive oil in a wok, then add the nuts and stir-fry over low heat for about 5 minutes, stirring all the time, until they begin to color.

4 Sprinkle the paprika and cumin over the nuts and continue stir-frying for an additional 1–2 minutes, or until nuts are golden brown.

5 Remove from the wok and drain on absorbent paper towels. Sprinkle with the salt, garnish with sprigs of cilantro, and serve hot or cold. If serving cold, store both the cheese appetizers and spicy nuts in airtight containers.

TASTY TIP

You can halve the quantities and serve with drinks as an appetizer at an informal dinner party for four to six people.

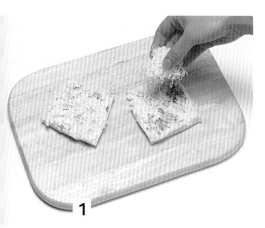
1

2

4

Quick Mediterranean Shrimp

INGREDIENTS

Serves 4

20 jumbo shrimp
3 tbsp. olive oil
1 garlic clove, peeled and crushed
2 tsp. finely grated lemon zest
1 tbsp. lemon juice
rosemary sprigs

For the pesto and sun-dried tomato dips:

²/₃ cup plain yogurt
1 tbsp. prepared pesto
²/₃ cup sour cream
1 tbsp. sun-dried tomato paste
1 tbsp. mustard
salt and freshly ground black pepper
lemon wedges, to garnish

HELPFUL HINT

Shrimp must always be cooked thoroughly, but you need to be careful not to overcook them or they will be tough. Remove from the refrigerator and leave at room temperature for about 15 minutes before stir-frying.

1 Remove the shells from the shrimp, leaving the tail shells. Using a small, sharp knife, remove the dark vein that runs along the back of the shrimp. Rinse and drain on absorbent paper towels.

2 Beat 2 tablespoons of the olive oil with the garlic, lemon zest, and juice in a small bowl. Bruise 1 sprig of rosemary with a rolling pin and add to the bowl. Add the shrimp, toss to coat, then cover and let marinate in the refrigerator until needed.

3 For the simple dips, mix the yogurt and pesto in one bowl and the sour cream, tomato paste, and mustard in another bowl. Season to taste with salt and pepper.

4 Heat a wok, add the remaining olive oil, and swirl around to coat the sides. Remove the shrimp from the marinade, leaving any juices and the rosemary behind. Add to the wok and stir-fry over high heat for 3–4 minutes, or until the shrimp are pink and just cooked through.

5 Remove the shrimp from the wok and arrange on a platter. Garnish with lemon wedges and more fresh rosemary sprigs, and serve hot or cold with the dips.

1

2

4

French Onion Tart

INGREDIENTS

Serves 4

Quick flaky pastry:

½ cup (1 stick) butter

1½ cups all-purpose flour

pinch of salt

For the filling:

2 tbsp. olive oil

4 large onions, peeled and
  thinly sliced

3 tbsp. white wine vinegar

2 tbsp. dark brown sugar

1½ cups grated cheddar cheese

a little beaten egg or milk

salt and freshly ground black pepper

TASTY TIP

For a milder, nutty taste, replace the cheddar cheese with Swiss cheese and grate a little nutmeg over the layer of cheese in step 4.

1 Preheat the oven to 400°F. Place the butter in the freezer for 30 minutes. Sift the flour and salt into a large bowl. Remove the butter from the freezer and grate, using the coarse side of a grater, dipping the butter in the flour every now and then to make it easier to grate.

2 Mix the butter into the flour using a knife, making sure that all of the butter is coated thoroughly with flour. Add 2 tablespoons cold water and continue to mix, bringing the mixture together. Use your hands to complete the mixing. Add a little more water if needed to leave a clean bowl. Place the pastry in a plastic bag and chill in the refrigerator for 30 minutes.

3 Heat the olive oil in a large skillet, then fry the onions for 10 minutes, stirring occasionally until softened. Stir in the white wine vinegar and sugar. Increase the heat and stir frequently, for another 4–5 minutes until the onions turn a deep caramel color. Cook for another 5 minutes, then set aside to cool.

4 On a lightly floured surface, roll out the pastry to a 14-inch circle. Wrap over a rolling pin and move the circle onto a cookie sheet. Sprinkle half the cheese over the pastry, leaving a 2-inch border around the edge, then spoon the caramelized onions over the cheese. Fold the uncovered pastry edges over the edge of the filling to form a rim, and brush the rim with beaten egg or milk.

5 Season to taste with salt and pepper. Sprinkle over the remaining cheddar cheese and bake for 20–25 minutes. Transfer to a large plate and serve immediately.

1

3

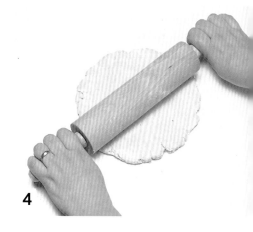

4

Parsnip Tart

INGREDIENTS

Serves 4

1 quantity quick flaky pastry
  (*see* page 152)

For the filling:

4 tbsp. butter
8 small parsnips, peeled
  and halved
1 tbsp. brown sugar
6 tbsp. apple juice

TASTY TIP

This dish is delicious when served warm with a Greek salad. Feta cheese is one of the main ingredients in Greek salad, and because of its salty content, it tastes particularly good with the creamy flavor of parsnips in this recipe.

1 Preheat the oven to 400°F. Heat the butter in an 8-inch skillet.

2 Add the parsnips, arranging the cut side down, with the narrow ends of the parsnips toward the center.

3 Sprinkle the parsnips with sugar and cook for 15 minutes, turning halfway through until golden.

4 Add the apple juice and bring to a boil. Remove the skillet from the heat.

5 On a lightly floured surface, roll the pastry out to a size slightly larger than the skillet.

6 Position the pastry over the parsnips and press down slightly to enclose the parsnips.

7 Bake in the preheated oven for 20–25 minutes until the parsnips and pastry are golden.

8 Invert a warm serving plate over the pan and carefully turn the pan over to flip the tart onto the plate. Serve immediately.

3

6

8

Garlic Wild Mushroom Galettes

INGREDIENTS

Serves 6

1 quantity quick flaky pastry
(*see* page 152), chilled
1 onion, peeled
1 red chile, seeded
2 garlic cloves, peeled
2½ cups mixed mushrooms (e.g.
oyster, crimini, morels, porcini,
and chanterelles)
2 tbsp. butter
2 tbsp. freshly chopped parsley
4 oz. mozzarella cheese, sliced

To serve:

cherry tomatoes
green salad

HELPFUL HINT

Many supermarkets stock a variety of wild mushrooms, all of which can be used in this recipe. It is important to maintain as much of the flavor of the mushrooms as possible, so do not peel mushrooms unless they appear old or tough.

1. Preheat the oven to 425°F. On a lightly floured surface, roll out the chilled pastry very thinly.

2. Cut out 6 circles about 6 inches in width and place on a lightly greased cookie sheet.

3. Thinly slice the onion, then divide into rings and set aside until needed.

4. Thinly slice the chile and slice the garlic into wafer-thin slivers. Add to the onion and set aside.

5. Wipe the mushrooms. Halve or quarter any large mushrooms and keep the small ones whole.

6. Heat the butter in a skillet, and sauté the onion, chile, and garlic gently for about 3 minutes. Add the mushrooms and cook for about 5 minutes, or until beginning to soften.

7. Stir the parsley into the mushroom mixture and drain off any excess liquid. Pile the mushroom mixture onto the pastry circles within ¼ inch of the edge. Arrange the sliced mozzarella cheese on top.

8. Bake in the preheated oven for 12–15 minutes, or until golden brown and serve with the tomatoes and salad.

2

5

7

Smoked Mackerel Vol-au-Vents

INGREDIENTS

Serves 1–2

¾ lb. prepared puff pastry

1 medium egg, beaten

2 tsp. sesame seeds

½ lb. peppered, smoked mackerel,
  skinned and chopped

2-in. piece cucumber

4 tbsp. cream cheese

2 tbsp. cranberry sauce

1 tbsp. freshly chopped dill

1 tbsp. finely grated lemon zest

dill sprigs, to garnish

mixed lettuce leaves, to serve

1 Preheat the oven to 450°F. Roll the pastry out on a lightly floured surface, and using a 3½-inch fluted cutter, cut out 12 circles.

2 Using a ½-inch cutter, mark a lid in the center of each circle.

3 Place on a damp cookie sheet and brush the circles with a little beaten egg.

4 Sprinkle the pastry with the sesame seeds, and bake in the preheated oven for 10–12 minutes, or until golden brown and well risen.

5 Transfer the vol-au-vents to a cutting board and, when cool enough to touch, carefully remove the lids with a small, sharp knife.

6 Scoop out any uncooked pastry from the inside of each vol-au-vent, then return to the oven for 5–8 minutes to dry out. Remove and cool.

7 Flake the mackerel into small pieces and set aside. Peel and dice the cucumber, and add to the mackerel.

8 Beat the cream cheese with the cranberry sauce, dill, and lemon zest. Stir in the mackerel and cucumber, and use to fill the vol-au-vents. Place the lids on top, and garnish with dill sprigs. Serve with lettuce leaves.

FOOD FACT

Mackerel is a relatively inexpensive and plentiful fish. Eating mackerel also provides one of the richest sources of minerals, oils, and vitamins available.

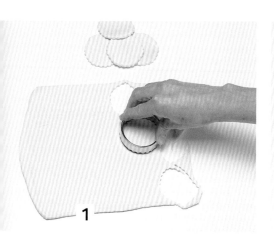

1

5

8

Olive & Feta Bundles

INGREDIENTS

Makes 30

1 small red bell pepper
1 small yellow bell pepper
²/₃ cup assorted marinated green and
  black olives
4 oz. feta cheese
2 tbsp. pine nuts,
  lightly toasted
6 sheets phyllo pastry
3 tbsp. olive oil
sour cream and chive dip,
  to serve

HELPFUL HINT

Feta is generally made from goat milk and has a salty taste. To make the cheese less salty simply soak in milk, then drain before eating.

1 Preheat the oven to 350°F. Preheat the broiler, then line the broiler rack with foil.

2 Cut the bell peppers into quarters and remove the seeds. Place skin-side up on the foil-lined broiler rack and cook under the preheated broiler for 10 minutes, turning occasionally until the skins begin to blacken.

3 Place the bell peppers in a plastic bag and leave until cool enough to handle, then peel and slice thinly.

4 Chop the olives and cut the feta cheese into small cubes. Mix the olives, feta, sliced bell peppers, and pine nuts together.

5 Cut 1 sheet of phyllo pastry in half, then brush with a little of the olive oil. Place a spoonful of the olive and feta mix one-third of the way up the pastry. Fold over the pastry and wrap to form a square package, encasing the filling completely.

6 Place this package in the center of the second half of the pastry sheet. Brush the edges lightly with a little olive oil, bring up the corners to meet in the center, and twist them loosely to form a pocket.

7 Brush with more olive oil and repeat with the remaining phyllo pastry and filling. Place the pockets on a lightly greased cookie sheet, and bake in the preheated oven for 10–15 minutes, or until crisp and golden. Serve with the dip.

2

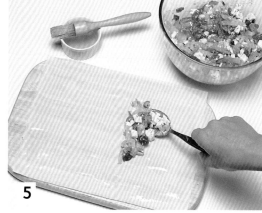

5

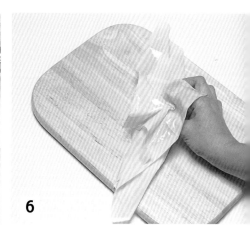

6

Antipasti with Focaccia

INGREDIENTS

Serves 4

3 fresh figs, quartered

²/₃ cup cooked and halved
  green beans

1 small head radicchio, rinsed
  and shredded

8–12 large shrimp, peeled
  and cooked

4 oz. canned sardines, drained

2 tbsp. pitted ripe olives

2 tbsp. stuffed green olives

1 cup sliced mozzarella cheese

1 cup thinly sliced Italian salami
  sausage

3 tbsp. olive oil

2¹/₂ cups high-gluten bread flour

pinch of sugar

1 cup fine semolina

1 tsp. salt

1¹/₄ tsp. rapid-rise active yeast

1¹/₄ cups warm water

a little extra olive oil for brushing

1 tbsp. coarse salt crystals

1 Preheat the oven to 425°F. Arrange the fresh figs, green beans, radicchio, shrimp, sardines, olives, mozzarella cheese, and slices of Italian salami on a large serving platter. Drizzle over 1 tablespoon of the olive oil, then cover with plastic wrap and chill in the refrigerator while making the bread.

2 To make the focaccia bread, sift the flour, sugar, semolina, and salt into a large mixing bowl, then sprinkle in the rapid-rise yeast. Make a well in the center and add the remaining 2 tablespoons of olive oil. Add the warm water, a little at a time, and mix together until a smooth, pliable dough is formed.

3 Place the dough onto a lightly floured board and knead until it is smooth and elastic. Place the dough in a lightly greased bowl, cover with a piece of plastic wrap, and leave in a warm place for 45 minutes.

4 Knead the dough again and flatten the dough into a large, flat oval shape, about ¹/₂ inch thick. Place the dough on a large, lightly greased baking sheet, and prick the surface with the end of a wooden spoon. Brush with olive oil and sprinkle with the coarse salt. Cook the bread in the preheated oven for about 25 minutes, or until it is golden brown. Serve the bread warm or cold with the prepared platter of food.

1

2

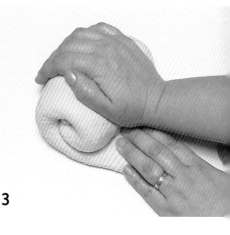

3

Mozzarella Frittata with Tomato & Basil Salad

INGREDIENTS

Serves 6

For the salad:

6 ripe but firm tomatoes
2 tbsp. fresh basil leaves
2 tbsp. olive oil
1 tbsp. fresh lemon juice
1 tsp. sugar
freshly ground black pepper

For the frittata:

7 large eggs, beaten
salt
$2^3/_4$ cups mozzarella cheese
2 scallions, trimmed and
   finely chopped
2 tbsp. olive oil
warm crusty bread, to serve

1   To make the tomato and basil salad, slice the tomatoes very thinly, tear the basil leaves, and sprinkle the basil over the tomatoes. Make the dressing by beating the olive oil, lemon juice, and sugar together. Season with pepper before drizzling the dressing over the salad.

2   To make the frittata, place the eggs in a large bowl with plenty of salt and beat. Shred the mozzarella and stir into the egg with the finely chopped scallions.

3   Preheat the broiler. Heat the olive oil in a nonstick ovenproof skillet and pour in the egg mixture, stirring with a wooden spoon to spread the ingredients evenly over skillet.

4   Broil for 5–8 minutes until the frittata is golden brown and firm on the underside. Place the whole skillet under the broiler, and cook for about 4–5 minutes, or until the top is golden brown. Slide the frittata onto a serving plate, cut into 6 large wedges, and serve immediately with the tomato and basil salad and plenty of warm crusty bread.

2

3

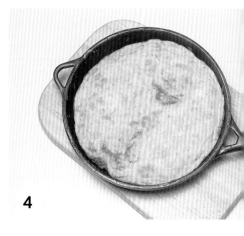

4

Fried Smelt with Arugula Salad

INGREDIENTS

Serves 4

1 lb. herring, fresh or frozen
vegetable oil, for deep-frying
³/₄ cup all-purpose flour
¹/₂ tsp. cayenne pepper
salt and freshly ground black pepper

For the salad:

2¹/₂ cups arugula
1 cup halved cherry tomatoes
³/₄ cup diced cucumber
3 tbsp. olive oil
1 tbsp. fresh lemon juice
¹/₂ tsp. mustard
¹/₂ tsp. sugar

TASTY TIP

Why not try a different salad? Mix together some baby spinach, cooked peas, and chopped scallions, then pour 2 tablespoons of garlic olive oil over the top. If serving with a chicken dish, top the salad with some feta or cheddar cheese.

1 If the herring are frozen, thaw completely, then wipe dry with absorbent paper towels.

2 Start to heat the vegetable oil in a deep fryer. Arrange the fish in a large, shallow dish and toss well in flour, cayenne pepper, salt, and pepper.

3 Deep-fry the fish in batches for 2–3 minutes, or until crisp and golden. Keep the cooked fish warm while deep-frying the remaining fish.

4 Meanwhile, to make the salad, arrange the arugula, cherry tomatoes, and cucumber on individual serving dishes. Beat the olive oil and the remaining ingredients together and season lightly. Drizzle the dressing over the salad and serve with the herring.

1

2

4

Bruschetta with Pecorino, Garlic & Tomatoes

INGREDIENTS

Serves 4

6 ripe but firm tomatoes
1 cup finely grated pecorino cheese
1 tbsp. oregano leaves
salt and freshly ground black pepper
3 tbsp. olive oil
3 garlic cloves, peeled
8 slices flat Italian bread, such
  as focaccia
8 thin slices mozzarella cheese
marinated ripe olives, to serve

TASTY TIP

Bitter lettuce is excellent with these bruschettas because they help to offset the richness of the cheese and tomato topping. Try a mixture of Italian red lettuce, radicchio, and arugula. If these are unavailable, use a bag of mixed lettuce.

1 Preheat the broiler and line the broiler rack with foil just before cooking. Make a small cross in the top of the tomatoes, then place in a small bowl and cover with boiling water. Let stand for 2 minutes, then drain and remove the skins. Cut into quarters, remove the seeds, and dice the flesh.

2 Mix the tomato flesh with the pecorino cheese and 2 teaspoons of the fresh oregano. Season to taste with salt and pepper. Add 1 tablespoon of the olive oil and mix thoroughly.

3 Crush the garlic and spread evenly over the slices of bread. Heat 2 tablespoons of the olive oil in a large skillet, and sauté the bread slices until they are crisp and golden.

4 Place the fried bread on a greased baking sheet and spoon on the tomato and cheese topping. Place some mozzarella on the top and place under the preheated broiler for 3–4 minutes until golden and bubbling. Garnish with the remaining oregano, then arrange the bruschettas on a serving plate and serve with the olives.

1

2

3

Crostini with Chicken Livers

INGREDIENTS

Serves 4

2 tbsp. olive oil

2 tbsp. butter

1 shallot, peeled and finely chopped

1 garlic clove, peeled and crushed

1½ cups chicken livers

1 tbsp. all-purpose flour

2 tbsp. dry white wine

1 tbsp. brandy

¼ cup sliced mushrooms

salt and freshly ground black pepper

4 slices ciabatta or similar bread

To garnish:

fresh sage leaves

lemon wedges

TASTY TIP

If you prefer a lower-fat alternative to the fried bread in this recipe, omit 1 tablespoon of the butter and brush the bread slices with the remaining 1 tablespoon of oil. Cook in a 350°F oven for about 20 minutes or until golden and crisp, then serve as above.

1 Heat 1 tablespoon of the olive oil and 1 tablespoon of the butter in a skillet, add the shallot and garlic, and cook gently for 2–3 minutes.

2 Trim and wash the chicken livers thoroughly and pat dry on absorbent paper towels as much as possible. Cut into slices, then toss in the flour. Add the livers to the skillet with the shallot and garlic, and continue to cook for an additional 2 minutes, stirring continuously.

3 Pour in the white wine and brandy, and bring to a boil. Boil rapidly for 1–2 minutes to allow the alcohol to evaporate, then stir in the sliced mushrooms and cook gently for about 5 minutes, or until the chicken livers are cooked but just a little pink inside. Season to taste with salt and pepper.

4 Cook the slices of ciabatta in the remaining oil and butter, then place on individual serving dishes. Spoon over the liver mixture and garnish with a few sage leaves and lemon wedges. Serve immediately.

2

3

3

Italian Baked Tomatoes with Frisée & Radicchio

INGREDIENTS

Serves 4

1 tsp. olive oil
4 large tomatoes
salt
½ cup fresh white bread crumbs
1 tbsp. freshly cut chives
1 tbsp. freshly chopped parsley
1 cup finely chopped baby
   mushrooms
salt and freshly ground black pepper
¼ cup freshly grated
   Parmesan cheese

For the salad:

½ head endive
½ small piece of radicchio
2 tbsp. olive oil
1 tsp. balsamic vinegar
salt and freshly ground black pepper

1. Preheat the oven to 375°F. Lightly grease a baking pan with the teaspoon of oil. Slice the tops off the tomatoes, remove all the tomato flesh, and strain into a large bowl. Sprinkle a little salt inside the tomato shells and then place them upside down on a plate while the filling is prepared.

2. Mix the strained tomatoes with the bread crumbs, fresh herbs, and mushrooms, and season well with salt and pepper. Place the tomato shells on the prepared baking sheet, and fill with the tomato-and-mushroom mixture. Sprinkle the cheese on the top and cook in the preheated oven for 15–20 minutes until golden brown.

3. Meanwhile, prepare the salad. Arrange the endive and radicchio on individual serving plates and mix the remaining ingredients together in a small bowl to make the dressing. Season to taste.

4. When the tomatoes are cooked, let rest for 5 minutes, then place on the prepared plates and drizzle over a little dressing. Serve warm.

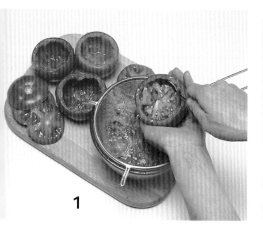

1

2

2

Spaghettini with Lemon Pesto & Cheese & Herb Bread

INGREDIENTS

Serves 4

1 small onion, peeled and grated

2 tsp. freshly chopped oregano

1 tbsp. freshly chopped parsley

6 tbsp. butter

1 cup grated pecorino cheese

8 slices Italian bread

3³/₄ cups dried spaghettini

¹/₄ cup olive oil

1 large bunch basil

³/₄ cup pine nuts

1 garlic clove, peeled and crushed

1 cup grated Parmesan cheese

2 tbsp. finely grated lemon zest

4 tbsp. lemon juice

salt and freshly ground black pepper

4 tsp. butter

1 Preheat the oven to 400°F. Mix together the onion, oregano, parsley, the 6 tablespoons of butter, and the cheese. Spread the bread with the cheese mixture, place on a lightly greased cookie sheet, and cover with foil. Cook in the preheated oven for 10–15 minutes, then keep warm.

2 Add the spaghettini and 1 tablespoon of olive oil to a large saucepan of fast-boiling, lightly salted water, and cook for 3–4 minutes, or until al dente. Drain and set aside 2 tablespoons of the cooking liquid aside.

3 Blend the basil, pine nuts, garlic, Parmesan cheese, lemon zest, lemon juice, and remaining olive oil in a food processor or blender until a puree is formed. Season to taste with salt and pepper, then place in a saucepan.

4 Heat the lemon pesto very gently until piping hot, then stir in the pasta and the cooking liquid. Add the 4 teaspoons butter and mix well together.

5 Add plenty of black pepper to the pasta and serve immediately with the warm cheese and herb bread.

1

3

4

Peperonata (Braised Mixed Peppers)

INGREDIENTS

Serves 4

2 green bell peppers
1 red bell pepper
1 yellow bell pepper
1 orange bell pepper
1 onion, peeled
2 garlic cloves, peeled
2 tbsp. olive oil
4 very ripe tomatoes
1 tbsp. freshly chopped oregano
salt and freshly ground black pepper
$^2/_3$ cup light chicken or
  vegetable stock
oregano sprigs, to garnish
focaccia (or flat bread), to serve

1 Remove the seeds from the bell peppers and cut into thin strips. Slice the onion into rings and chop the garlic cloves finely.

2 Heat the olive oil in a skillet and cook the peppers, onions, and garlic for 5–10 minutes, or until soft and lightly browned. Stir continuously.

3 Make a cross on the top of the tomatoes, then place in a bowl and cover with boiling water. Let stand for about 2 minutes. Drain, then remove the skins and seeds, and chop the tomato flesh into cubes.

4 Add the tomatoes and oregano to the bell peppers and onion, and season to taste with salt and pepper. Cover the skillet and bring to a boil. Reduce the heat and simmer gently for about 30 minutes, or until tender, adding the stock halfway through the cooking time.

5 Garnish with sprigs of oregano and serve hot with plenty of freshly cooked focaccia bread.

TASTY TIP

Serve the peperonata cold as part of an antipasti platter. Some good accompaniments would be marinated olives, sun-dried or semidried marinated tomatoes, sliced salamis and other cold meats, and plenty of Italian bread.

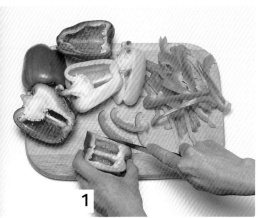
1

2

4

Hot Jumbo Shrimp with Prosciutto

INGREDIENTS

Serves 4

½ cucumber, peeled

4 ripe tomatoes

12 jumbo shrimp

6 tbsp. olive oil

4 garlic cloves, peeled and crushed

4 tbsp. freshly chopped parsley

salt and freshly ground black pepper

6 slices prosciutto, cut in half

4 slices Italian bread

½ cup dry white wine

HELPFUL HINT

The black intestinal vein needs to be removed from raw shrimp because it can cause a bitter flavor. Remove the shell, then using a small, sharp knife, make a cut along the center back of the shrimp and open out the flesh. Using the tip of the knife, remove the thread that lies along the length of the shrimp, and discard.

1 Preheat the oven to 350°F. Slice the cucumber and tomatoes thinly, then arrange on 4 large plates and set aside. Peel the shrimp, leaving the tail shell intact, and remove the thin black vein running down the back.

2 Beat together 4 tablespoons of the olive oil, the garlic, and chopped parsley in a small bowl, and season to taste with plenty of salt and pepper. Add the shrimp to the mixture, and stir until they are well coated. Remove the shrimp, then wrap each one in a piece of prosciutto and secure with a toothpick.

3 Place the prepared shrimp on a lightly greased baking sheet or dish with the slices of bread, and cook in the preheated oven for 5 minutes.

4 Remove the shrimp from the oven and spoon the wine over the shrimp and bread. Return to the oven and cook for an additional 10 minutes until piping hot.

5 Carefully remove the toothpicks and arrange 3 shrimp rolls on each slice of bread. Place on top of the sliced cucumber and tomatoes, and serve immediately.

2

2

4

Mozzarella Pockets with Cranberry Relish

INGREDIENTS

Serves 6

For the mozzarella pockets:

1 cup mozzarella cheese
8 slices white bread
2 large eggs, beaten
salt and freshly ground black pepper
1 cup olive oil

For the relish:

1 cup cranberries
2 tbsp. fresh orange juice
2 tsp. grated orange zest
¼ cup brown sugar
1 tbsp. port or fortified wine

HELPFUL HINT

Frying in oil that is not hot enough causes food to absorb more oil than it would if fried at the correct heat. To test the temperature of the oil without a thermometer, drop a cube of bread into the skillet. If the bread browns in 30 seconds, the oil is at the right temperature.

1. Slice the mozzarella thinly, remove the crusts from the bread, and make sandwiches with the bread and cheese. Cut into 2-inch squares and press them flat. Season the eggs with salt and pepper, then soak the bread in the seasoned egg for 1 minute on each side until well coated.

2. Heat the olive oil to 375°F and deep-fry the bread squares for 1–2 minutes or until they are crisp and golden brown. Drain on absorbent paper towels and keep warm.

3. Place the cranberries, orange juice, zest, sugar, and port or wine into a small saucepan, and add 5 tablespoons water. Bring to a boil, then reduce the heat and simmer for 10 minutes, or until the cranberries have "popped." Sweeten with a little more sugar, if necessary.

4. Arrange the mozzarella pockets on individual serving plates. Serve with some of the cranberry relish.

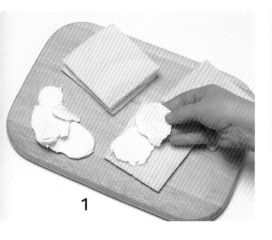

1

1

3

Beet Ravioli with Dill Cream Sauce

INGREDIENTS

Serves 4–6

For the pasta dough:

2 cups bread flour or type 00 pasta
  flour, plus extra for rolling
1 tsp. salt
2 large eggs
1 large egg yolk
1 tbsp. extra virgin olive oil

For the filling:

1 tbsp. olive oil
1 small onion, peeled and
  finely chopped
½ tsp. caraway seeds
1 cup chopped cooked beets
6 oz. ricotta cheese
½ cup fresh white bread crumbs
1 large egg yolk
2 tbsp. grated Parmesan cheese
salt and freshly ground black pepper

For the sauce:

4 tbsp. walnut oil
4 tbsp. freshly chopped dill
1 tbsp. green peppercorns, drained
  and coarsely chopped
6 tbsp. crème fraîche

1 Sift the flour and salt into a large bowl. Make a well in the center and add the eggs and yolk, oil, and 1 teaspoon water. Gradually mix to form a soft (but not sticky) dough, adding a little more flour or water as necessary. Transfer to a lightly floured surface and knead for 5 minutes, or until smooth and elastic. Cover with plastic wrap and let rest at room temperature for about 30 minutes.

2 For the filling, heat the olive oil in a large skillet. Add the onion and caraway seeds, and cook over medium heat for 5 minutes, or until the onion is softened and lightly golden. Stir in the beets and cook for 5 minutes. Blend the mixture in a food processor until smooth, then let cool. Stir in the ricotta, bread crumbs, egg yolk, and Parmesan cheese. Season the filling to taste with salt and pepper and set aside.

3 Divide the pasta dough into 8 pieces. Roll out flat into rectangles. Lay 1 sheet on a floured surface and place 5 heaping teaspoons of the filling 1 inch apart. Dampen the dough around the heaps of filling and lay a second sheet of pasta over the top. Press around the heaps to seal. Cut into squares using a pastry wheel or sharp knife. Put the filled pasta shapes onto a floured dish towel.

4 Bring a large pan of lightly salted water to a rolling boil. Drop the ravioli into the boiling water, return to a boil, and cook for 3–4 minutes until al dente.

5 Meanwhile, heat the walnut oil in a small saucepan, then add the chopped dill and green peppercorns. Remove from the heat, stir in the crème fraîche, and season well. Drain the cooked pasta thoroughly and toss with the sauce. Spoon onto warmed serving dishes and serve immediately.

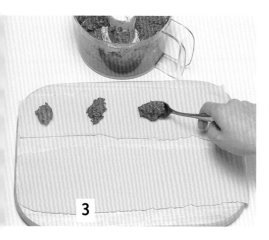

3

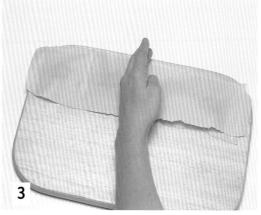

3

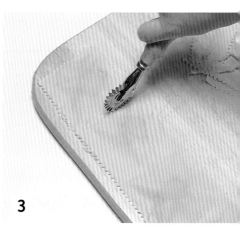

3

Gnocchi with Broiled Cherry Tomato Sauce

INGREDIENTS

Serves 4

1 lb. mealy potatoes, unpeeled

1 large egg

1 tsp. salt

about ³/₄ cup all-purpose flour

1 lb. mixed red and orange cherry
   tomatoes, halved lengthwise

2 garlic cloves, peeled and
   finely sliced

finely grated zest of ¹/₂ lemon

1 tbsp. freshly chopped thyme

1 tbsp. freshly chopped basil

2 tbsp. extra virgin olive oil

salt and freshly ground black pepper

pinch of sugar

freshly grated Parmesan cheese,
   to serve

HELPFUL HINT

When cooking the gnocchi, use a
very large pan with at least 8 cups of
water to give them plenty of room
so that they do not stick together.

1 Preheat the broiler just before cooking. Bring a large pan of salted water to a boil. Add the potatoes and cook for 20–25 minutes until tender. Drain. Leave until cool enough to handle but still hot, then peel them and place in a large bowl. Mash until smooth, then work in the egg, salt, and enough of the flour to form a soft dough.

2 With floured hands, roll a spoonful of the dough into a small ball. Flatten the ball slightly onto the back of a large fork, then roll it off the fork to make a little ridged dumpling. Place each gnocchi on a floured dish towel as you work.

3 Place the tomatoes in a flameproof shallow dish. Add the garlic, lemon zest, herbs, and olive oil. Season to taste with salt and pepper, and sprinkle over the sugar. Cook under the preheated broiler for 10 minutes, or until the tomatoes are charred and tender, stirring once or twice.

4 Meanwhile, bring a large pan of lightly salted water to a boil, then reduce to a steady simmer. Dropping in 6–8 gnocchi at a time, cook in batches for 3–4 minutes or until they begin bobbing up to the surface. Remove with a slotted spoon and drain well on paper towels before transferring to a warmed serving dish; cover with foil. Toss the cooked gnocchi with the tomato sauce. Serve immediately with a little grated Parmesan cheese.

1

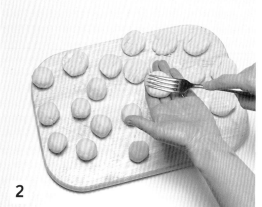

2

4

Tiny Pasta with Fresh Herb Sauce

INGREDIENTS

Serves 6

3¼ cups tripolini (small bows with
   rounded ends) or small farfalle
2 tbsp. freshly chopped Italian
   flat-leaf parsley
2 tbsp. freshly chopped basil
1 tbsp. freshly snipped chives
1 tbsp. freshly chopped chervil
1 tbsp. freshly chopped tarragon
1 tbsp. freshly chopped sage
1 tbsp. freshly chopped oregano
1 tbsp. freshly chopped marjoram
1 tbsp. freshly chopped thyme
1 tbsp. freshly chopped rosemary
finely grated zest of 1 lemon
5 tbsp. extra virgin olive oil
2 garlic cloves, peeled and
   finely chopped
½ tsp. dried chili flakes
salt and freshly ground black pepper
freshly grated Parmesan cheese,
   to serve

1 Bring a large pan of lightly salted water to a rolling boil. Add the pasta and cook according to the package directions, or until al dente.

2 Meanwhile, place all the herbs, lemon zest, olive oil, garlic, and chile flakes in a heavy pan. Heat gently for 2–3 minutes, or until the herbs turn bright green and become very fragrant. Remove from the heat and season to taste with salt and pepper.

3 Drain the pasta thoroughly, setting aside 2–3 tablespoons of the cooking water. Transfer the pasta to a large serving bowl.

4 Pour the heated herb mixture over the pasta and toss together until thoroughly mixed. Check and adjust the seasoning, adding a little of the pasta cooking water if the pasta mixture seems a bit dry. Transfer to warmed serving dishes and serve immediately with grated Parmesan cheese.

2

3

4

Louisiana Shrimp & Fettuccine

INGREDIENTS

Serves 4

4 tbsp. olive oil

1 lb. jumbo shrimp, washed and
   peeled, shells and heads set aside

2 shallots, peeled and finely chopped

4 garlic cloves, peeled and
   finely chopped

large handful fresh basil leaves

1 carrot, peeled and finely chopped

1 onion, peeled and finely chopped

1 celery stalk, trimmed and
   finely chopped

2–3 parsley sprigs

2–3 thyme sprigs

salt and freshly ground black pepper

pinch of cayenne pepper

$^3/_4$ cup dry white wine

2 cups coarsely chopped,
   ripe tomatoes

juice of $^1/_2$ lemon, or to taste

12 oz. fettuccine

1 Heat 2 tablespoons of the olive oil in a large pan and add the shrimp shells and heads. Fry over high heat for 2–3 minutes until the shells turn pink and are lightly browned. Add half the shallots, half the garlic, half the basil, and the carrot, onion, celery, parsley, and thyme. Season lightly with salt, pepper, and cayenne, and fry for 2–3 minutes, stirring often.

2 Pour in the wine and stir, scraping the pan well. Bring to a boil, reduce the heat and simmer for 1 minute, then add the tomatoes. Cook for an additional 3–4 minutes, then pour in $^3/_4$ cup water. Bring to a boil, reduce the heat, and simmer for about 30 minutes, stirring often and using a wooden spoon to mash the shrimp shells in order to release as much flavor as possible into the sauce. Lower the heat if the sauce is reducing very quickly.

3 Strain through a strainer, pressing well to extract as much liquid as possible; there should be about 1$^1/_2$ cups. Pour the liquid into a clean pan and bring to a boil, then lower the heat and simmer gently until the liquid is reduced by about half.

4 Heat the remaining olive oil over high heat in a clean skillet and add the peeled shrimp. Season lightly and add the lemon juice. Cook for 1 minute, reduce the heat, and add the remaining shallots and garlic. Cook for 1 minute. Add the sauce and adjust the seasoning.

5 Meanwhile, bring a large pan of lightly salted water to a rolling boil and add the fettuccine. Cook according to the package directions, or until al dente, and drain thoroughly. Transfer to a warmed serving dish. Add the sauce and toss well. Garnish with the remaining basil and serve immediately.

Gnocchetti with Broccoli & Bacon Sauce

INGREDIENTS

Serves 6

1 lb. broccoli florets

4 tbsp. olive oil

½ cup finely chopped pancetta or
smoked bacon

1 small onion, peeled and
finely chopped

3 garlic cloves, peeled and sliced

¾ cup milk

4 cups gnocchetti (little elongated
ribbed shells)

½ cup freshly grated Parmesan
cheese, plus extra to serve

salt and freshly ground black pepper

FOOD FACT

Pancetta is an Italian bacon that may be either smoked or unsmoked. You can buy it sliced or in a piece, but it is often sold prepacked, cut into tiny cubes ready for cooking. Thickly cut, smoked bacon makes a good alternative.

1   Bring a large pan of salted water to a boil. Add the broccoli florets and cook for about 8–10 minutes, or until very soft. Drain thoroughly and let cool slightly; then chop finely and set aside.

2   Heat the olive oil in a heavy pan. Add the pancetta or bacon and cook over medium heat for 5 minutes, or until golden and crisp. Add the onion and cook for an additional 5 minutes, or until soft and lightly golden. Add the garlic and cook for 1 minute.

3   Transfer the chopped broccoli to the bacon or pancetta mixture and pour in the milk. Bring slowly to a boil, reduce the heat, and simmer rapidly for about 15 minutes, or until reduced to a creamy texture.

4   Meanwhile, bring a large pan of lightly salted water to a rolling boil. Add the pasta and cook according to the package directions, or until al dente.

5   Drain the pasta thoroughly, setting aside a little of the cooking water. Add the pasta and the Parmesan cheese to the broccoli mixture. Toss, adding enough of the cooking water to make a creamy sauce. Season to taste with salt and pepper. Serve immediately with extra Parmesan cheese.

1

2

3

Index